**Creative Id
the Family E**

This book is dedicated to my mother,
Daphne Lenton

Creative Ideas for the Family Eucharist

Sarah Lenton

Theological consultant:
Andrew Davison

CANTERBURY PRESS
Norwich

© Sarah Lenton, 2022

First published in 2022 by the Canterbury Press Norwich
Editorial office
3rd Floor, Invicta House
108–114 Golden Lane
London EC1Y 0TG, UK

www.canterburypress.co.uk

Canterbury Press is an imprint of Hymns Ancient & Modern Ltd
(a registered charity)

Ancient & Modern

Hymns Ancient & Modern® is a registered trademark of
Hymns Ancient & Modern Ltd
13A Hellesdon Park Road, Norwich,
Norfolk NR6 5DR, UK

All rights reserved. No part of this publication may be reproduced,
stored in a retrieval system, or transmitted,
in any form or by any means, electronic, mechanical,
photocopying or otherwise, without the prior permission of
the publisher, Canterbury Press.

The Author has asserted her right under the Copyright, Designs and Patents Act 1988 to be identified as the Author of this Work

British Library Cataloguing in Publication data

A catalogue record for this book is available
from the British Library

978 1 84825 530 2

Typeset by Regent Typesetting
Printed and bound in Great Britain by
CPI Group (UK) Ltd, Croydon

Contents

Acknowledgements	7
Introduction	9
General Principles	12
Setting up a Family Eucharist	31
The Eucharist Step by Step	41

THE SCRIPTS

Script 1 – Advent Sunday (Advent Gospels)	1
Script 2 – St John the Baptist	6
Script 3 – Christmas Crackers (Christmas Day Script 1)	10
Script 4 – Christmas Tree (Christmas Day Script 2)	14
Script 5 – Speaking Animals (Christmas Day Script 3)	19
Script 6 – The Naming of Jesus (The Naming and Circumcision of Jesus)	23
Script 7 – The Holy Family	27
Script 8 – The Three Gifts (Epiphany Script 1)	31
Script 9 – Useful Presents (Epiphany Script 2)	36
Script 10 – The Baptism of Our Lord in a Family Eucharist that includes Holy Baptism	40
Script 11 – Candles (The Presentation of Jesus in the Temple Script 1)	44
Script 12 – Christingle (The Presentation of Jesus in the Temple Script 2)	49
Script 13 – The Annunciation	53
Script 14 – Ash Wednesday	58
Script 15 – Lent	62
Script 16 – The Transfiguration	67
Script 17 – Mothering Sunday (Lent 4 Script 1) (Using the Gospel of the Prodigal Son)	70
Script 18 – Mothering Sunday (Lent 4 Script 2)	74

Script 19 – Holy Week	77
Script 20 – Finding Jesus (Easter Day Script 1)	79
Script 21 – The Paschal Candle (Easter Day Script 2)	83
Script 22 – Opening and Closing (Easter Day Script 3)	88
Script 23 – Rock and Roll (Easter Day Script 4)	92
Script 24 – Eastertide (The Walk to Emmaus)	96
Script 25 – Ascension Day	100
Script 26 – Pentecost	104
Script 27 – Trinity Sunday	108
Script 28 – Bread from Heaven (Corpus Christi)	112
Script 29 – The Feasts of Saints Peter and Paul (29 June)	116
Script 30 – The Assumption (15 August)	123
Script 31 – St Michael and All Angels (29 September)	128
Script 32 – All Souls (31 October)	133
Script 33 – Jigsaw Man (All Saints Day – 1 November)	136
Script 34 – Christ the King	139
Script 35 – The Rich Fool (Harvest)	143

Appendixes

Eucharistic Prayer H	149
Children's Liturgy for Good Friday	151
Children's Mass	156
Intercessions	163
Stations of the Cross	178

Acknowledgements

This book started life six years ago, and my first debt of gratitude must be to the Canterbury Press for waiting, and particularly to Christine Smith, Publishing Director, who suggested I expand a simple sermon list into a book for the Family Eucharist, even though it added some years to the process.

As it is a Family Eucharist book, I am very grateful to the churches, clergy and children who have let me try my ideas on them, particularly Fr Kevin Morris at St Michael and All Angels, Bedford Park, London, and the Liturgy Team at Our Lady of Lourdes, Acton.

Even heavier is the debt I owe to the friends who bashed out the sessions with me, improved them, acted in them and were living proof of Our Lord's idea that disciples act better together in twos and threes. Practically any reference to Pauline theology can be attributed to the Revd Dr Melanie Marshall (along with the discovery that all three kings brought chocolate to the crib). Fr Tito Pereira's profound belief that small children are natural metaphysicians was a constant inspiration – as well as his ability to send pithy theological texts in any crisis. The Revd Dr Andrew Davison, who encouraged me to write in the first place, has ensured that the theology and liturgy are both orthodox and accessible. Any errors that have crept in, in spite of these excellent mentors, are entirely my fault.

The generous team of photographers who record the year at St Michael's have again allowed me to use their pictures, and I offer a huge thank you to David Beresford, Jim Cox, Lawrence Brooks and Kelvin Murray. I don't know how I can ever thank Margaret Stonborough adequately – she was not only the prop maker, stage manager and 'stooge' in some of the routines, but laid out the entire book from its very earliest stages. And nothing at all could have been done without my family, particularly my sister Jane Trigle, who always laughs at my jokes – and contributes a fair amount of her own – and my mother, to whom I have dedicated this book, and who taught me to pray and to love the Lord in the first place.

Introduction

Family services: one of the most important things we do as a church and one of the most difficult. How do we get children involved in regular worship? We can *accommodate* them – with colouring books, or Sunday school – but how do we get them to stick out a whole service? That's the challenge this book sets out to address.

If the most fundamental problem is 'How am I going to keep a load of kids engaged for the next hour?', it's swiftly followed by others: 'How – given the noise, toys, and child-friendly music – are the other "ages" in "All Age Worship" going to worship at all?' Should we move the front pews? Is this the moment to invest in an overhead projector? What do we do with the buggies? But the first decision must be, 'What sort of service will this be?'

This book assumes it's going to be a Family Eucharist. (See page 62 for notes on a non-Eucharist service.)

Family Eucharist[1]

All Age Eucharist – or a Family Mass – is simply the regular parish communion service on Sunday angled towards accessibility to children as well as adults. This means cancelling Sunday school and putting away the colouring books so that everyone worships in church together for the duration of the liturgy.

---

1 Mass or Holy Communion. All three titles of the central act of Christian worship will be used as we describe the traditional liturgy of the Western Church.

This book offers guidelines on how to run a Family Eucharist, work with children, ad lib fearlessly, and provides a sermon suitable for kids and adults for each major feast of the Christian year. It draws its inspiration from two areas of my working life – the theatre and my parish church. The theatre first ...

Theatre

My first encounter with children's worship was in a small hall attached to the local Catholic church. It was jammed with 75 kids and the noise was indescribable. But, to my amazement, the moment the leader bellowed 'In the Name of the Father ...' utter silence fell as the children made the Sign of the Cross and finished the prayer. There was a fractional pause after the Amen, and the leader jumped in. He knew his audience, he knew the opening line – and he had the next line ready.

Even so, we lost the kids after ten minutes and I began to think that the problem was theatrical: we didn't have a script, or anyone on hand to pick up a cue, run with a story, or vary the pace. We were in fact totally lacking in stagecraft. I went home to my drawing desk and started to sketch all the things one needs to put on a show. And looking at them, I thought they were basically transferable to a kids' service.[2]

---

2 One can push this too far: the Eucharist is supremely an act of worship, *Carmen* is not. Even so, the tie-up between church and stage is not limited to practical matters like props. Professionalism, integrity and belief in the show, are crucial to priest and performer alike.

The stage, audience and props can be re-labelled sanctuary steps, congregation and – well – props. The main performer is the preacher (who may also be the vicar) while the rest of the cast are the crucial people needed to run a family service. Front of House is easy – that will be a helpful parent who sits with the audience and keeps an eye out for toddlers in distress. The techie and other performer can be the curate, another parent, or a helpful teenager – anyone you can rely on to pick up a cue and hand over a prop. (The importance of the second person is discussed on pages 32–33.) And with these in place, all you need is a script.

The scripts

The sermons in this book are presented in the form of play scripts – that is, they give the preacher his or her 'lines'. The text includes the dialogue you have with the kids, gags, pictures, gestures, and the role of your helper and/or stooge (the scripts assume that anyone involved in the sermon – except the preacher – won't see their 'part' until ten minutes before the service).

You don't need to be a great performer for these scripts to work; run them straight and they'll do the job. The laughs are pretty much guaranteed, as are the probable responses from the children. Most of the text bounces off props and interaction so, though it's fine to deliver the sermon with the script in hand, once you've got the props in the right order, you'll find it quite easy to ad lib.

The preacher is assumed to be the vicar but actually anyone can do this, as long as they present well, and are alive to the particular challenge of a family service. That's because a Family Eucharist is not the ordinary Sunday service, with a kids' sermon tacked on;[3] it's a liturgy that includes children – and their families – from the opening procession to the final dismissal. And bang in the middle of the action is the sermon. It's the turning point of the service, the moment when we move from the Liturgy of the Word to the Liturgy of the Eucharist: the springboard, bouncing the kids into the second half of Mass, and helping them to make the transition from being listeners to participants.

Online resources

For cartoons and supporting resources for the book, please visit www.canterburypress.co.uk/downloads.

---

[3] Nor is it a children's service. The fun of family services is trying to keep the grown-ups on board as well.

General Principles

The first thing to do is ease up …

Space for Babies

This doesn't mean checking in all the robes and candlesticks – these are positive assets in a family service – but it does mean elbow room. New families are more likely to relax when they realize they can move around, and even disappear, easily. If you have a side room, arrange crèche facilities for crying babies and their agitated parents. Once the child has calmed down, encourage them back into church. Ask some of your regulars to walk their babies up and down during the service to give the newcomers the confidence to do the same.

Babies often respond to a sacred atmosphere

Make it clear that the church space is as much for the kids as the adults: set aside an aisle or the back of the church for prams and buggies – and don't mind or react if smaller children talk or play during the service. They won't get it all at once and they don't need to: it's much more important that they have a good experience of coming to church.

The only kid who doesn't wriggle in church is Baby Jesus …

Space for Adults

Some adults may need extra attention in a family service: alert the sidespeople to the needs of Mrs so-and-so who always sits in the same pew, and don't be fazed by total newcomers who walk in and, thinking the service is just for kids, sit at the back with a café latte and a newspaper. Hand them a service book anyway and let them work it out.

Working with Children

All church services are implicitly 'all age' services, so what makes an 'All Age' service different? Practically speaking, it's the emphasis on engagement with children, so the first thing to do is develop a rapport with the younger members of your congregation.

Nothing beats actually liking children – or acting as if you do. If you have a chance, go and see a good reception teacher at work. You can follow the rules of thumb below, but watching a professional at work will give you a sense of interaction, body language, and some useful tips on getting the kids' attention.

Think about the sort of things children like. A brainstorming session with some parents produced the following: food, games, stories, wrapped presents, horror stories, ghastly jokes, puzzles, rules (oddly enough), ritual, questions (particularly easy questions), applause, noise, huddling together and jumping about. The point of the list is not to see what you can incorporate into a family service, but to get yourself into a child's mindset. Children turn out to like practically everything – which makes them very easy to please – and the bare mention of grub brings an alert look to all the little eyes present. Also, children will go more than halfway to please you. They want to be friends.

> ### *Ghouls and other horrors*
>
> **The Bible has its share of ghoulishness and we've found it better for kids to be allowed to relish, say, the ten plagues of Egypt in church, rather than slope off and download horror games at home.**
>
> (See page 133 for a sermon on Hallowe'en.)

Realism

Having said that, you have to allow for a kid's attention span (one minute per year of age apparently), the fact that they get over-excited, may prefer to play with some hard noisy toy and that, however brilliant you are, there'll always be someone who's switched off for a moment.[4]

The only way to address this is rapport. You can't start a dialogue with over 20 kids at once, but you can *look* as if you're doing so. Start off by making sure you can be seen. It sounds obvious, but don't stand behind the altar, or in a sideways position in a choir stall – go up a level, or move forward towards the congregation.

Getting the Audience's Attention

Catching their eye,   using a prop,   or a head mike ...

---

4 Stand-up comics have to learn not to get fixated on the one member of the audience who doesn't laugh – a 90 per cent success rate is excellent.

Learn your opening sentence so you can look straight at the children, and then bounce off to look at the adults – they need to know you are addressing them as well. Give the kids something to do. It might be as simple as asking them to stand up, or make the Sign of the Cross ✠ (see page 42), or answering a very easy question:

> Hands up anyone here who's ever had a birthday?

Stagger back at the response

> What, all of you?
> Well, today we're going to hear about (*the birthday of St John the Baptist or whatever the follow-up is*)

The major interaction between you and the kids will happen at the sermon. Encourage the children to come down to the front for this. (You may *really* need to encourage them; don't say it once and carry on.) A major reason for having them down the front is to detach them from their parents – they behave better without them – however, the very small (and shy) often feel happier if they can bring Mum or Dad along as well, so you'll probably find a scattering of adults sitting among the children.

Such parents are very useful – they follow the story, laugh at the jokes, and alert you to the fact that little Joe has had his hand up for the last ten minutes.

On the floor

Down the front means sitting on the floor. Don't worry about this, children are bendier than us. They are used to the floor from school assembly, and are mysteriously better behaved down there. Children on chairs don't bond as an audience – they tend to swing about, and kick the chair (or the child) in front. Also, no chairs means you've got free space for you and the children to move about if the sermon takes a dramatic form. Sheep snaffling, for example …

Children are used to clear instructions, and – in all but the most disruptive cases – will follow them. Don't be afraid to tell them when to sit, stand, turn to a partner, etc. You can't be too simple – especially as there are bound to be under-5s present, who will need to be told every step of a sequence. So, before a story or the sermon, develop a patter that will tell them what's going to happen, where they should sit, which way to face, and generally gets them ready to listen. Something like this …

> OK, we're going to listen to a story.
> I'd like all the kids to come down to the front …
> Thanks!
> Right, watch me, can you *(use a hand movement)* sit down?
> Brilliant!

Or if it's not …

> Useless!
> Jump up, let's try again. Watch my hand *(use the same gesture)* – sit!
> Fantastic.

Start the sermon/story by holding up a prop or drawing a picture (see the scripts below; don't worry about drawing – templates are provided). If the kids are making a noise, look cheerful, and go quiet. This requires some nerve. Thank the kids who settle down, by name: 'Thanks, Charlie, that's really quiet' or 'Well done, Tina …'

If the children are about to pray, run a really simple sequence:

> We're going to pray together.
> Let's sit quietly.
> Face the front – can you see me?
> Can anyone show me how we pray?

Some child is bound to put his/her hands together

> Perfect! Well done, Bella.
> We put our hands together.

Do so

> And sit very still.

You'll now have time for a short prayer. Children usually like repeating phrases after you. If it's very quiet you may feel you can risk a minute's devotion. One way to get children ready for that is to say:

> Can you put your hands on your chest – like this …

Do so yourself

> Shut your eyes.
> Can you feel your hand?
> That's how close God is to you.
> Let's talk to Him now.

Or you could ask them to watch as somebody lights a prayer candle, or holds up a picture. Suggest things they may like to think about – how quietly the flame flickers, how interested God is in the things we tell Him.

If you manage a minute you've done well. End the second you think you're losing them with an **Amen**. (And ask a child to blow out the candle.)

Adults

Get into the habit of asking the adults to join in. In the pews the children will instantly notice if Mum or Dad are detached, and conclude that praying, etc. is something for little kids. Down at the front, the grown-ups in your team should show the kids how to pray by doing it themselves.

Channelling Energy

Break up the service into manageable chunks (see page 22), vary the pace, and build in physical activities. Naturally children want to move or jump around – so do grown-ups; it's why so many adults enjoy processions and the Stations of the Cross. Just getting the kids to charge down to the front for the sermon will please them …

But you can do better than that. There's no reason why a kid pretending to be an aeroplane can't be turned into something more obviously liturgical. You can run a whole session on useful and useless stances for prayer.

> O Lord, who knowest … that by reason of the frailty of our nature we cannot always stand upright …
> (*Collect for the fourth Sunday after Epiphany*).

There's a Ready Steady Pray! session on page 1, or the children can learn the Sign of the Cross in several bizarre ways (page 42). They can bow, and genuflect, and give the Peace. They can jump up at Easter to symbolize the Resurrection; they can stand and turn on the spot to illustrate the meaning of the word 'repent'; and they can address the whole church in a massed chorus. There are so many things you can teach the children (and, by extension, the congregation) to do that you may want to limit them to one new gesture per service.

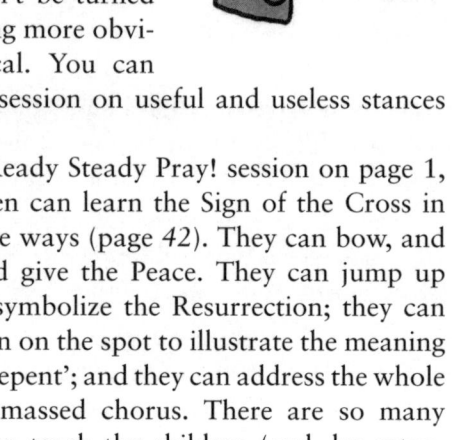

Things to Play With

An obvious way to stop the children mucking around with toy cars is to give them holy things to play with instead. With a little practice, they can be taught to ring hand bells in a seemly fashion in the Eucharistic Prayer, or they can surround the Gospel holding candles or fake tea lights (the battery-operated sort you get at garden centres). Practically any ordinary toy can be commandeered to illustrate a sermon and the church prop box should fill up relatively soon with pirate treasure, helmets, crowns, handcuffs and the attributes of saints (which can of course be anything – plastic scythes, large keys, eyeballs from the joke shop, and so on). Many props can be made on the day – a DIY yoke, for example (see Script 29).

The more august props used in church – the aspergillum, the vessels used for the Elements, and supremely (from the glamour point of view) the incense boat and thurible – need to be held in reserve. Children are usually deeply interested in these objects, but mainly because they are so odd and holy. There is a section on catholic aids to worship below.

Interacting with the Children

All the scripts below assume that you will be near enough the kids to interact with them. They may come up to help you finish a picture, smell the oil of Chrism – and they'll certainly want to answer your questions. All school-age children know about putting their hand up, try to stick with this and discourage shouting out. Fortunately, the lovely thing about church is that it *isn't* school, and there's no reason why the kids shouldn't be asked appallingly easy questions. Sophisticated

12-year-olds have no objection to telling everyone what red on a traffic light signifies.

When a child does give an answer, immediately repeat it so that the whole congregation can hear. (Don't do this if a child says something comically inappropriate, however funny or endearing. The idea is not to make comic mileage out of the children themselves, and it derails the script.)

You won't be able to give everyone a chance to shine and, when children are getting frantic at not being asked, eyeball them sympathetically: 'You knew that, didn't you, William?' Another strategy is to say, 'How many of you were going to say that?' and react suitably to the forest of hands. Very small children put up their hands just for the fun of it and are quite content with a 'Hello, Rory!' as the preacher moves on.

Interacting with the Adults

Throw some questions open to the adults, especially if the kids go quiet – 'Does anyone out there know?' For some sermons you'll find it helpful to have an ally who doesn't mind having the laugh turned against them, or can be relied on to answer back. Have you got a biblical whizz in your church? Or someone with an exciting job, like a tube driver, or an athlete? One of the ladies in the choir once corrected me for getting the number of *The Flying Scotsman* wrong – that is just the sort of heckling you want.

You'll probably find that things you put on for the kids, like egg rolling, will delight most adults as well.

Keeping the Congregation on Board

In a Family Mass you can more or less count on the co-operation of the parents and children – but what about the regulars? Basically you have to throw yourself on their generosity. We are heirs to Jesus' unique appreciation of children and, though it's a privilege to follow His lead, it's unwise to assume the text 'Suffer little children …' will carry all before it.

> He called a child, whom He put among them, and said, 'Truly I tell you, unless you change and become like children, you will never enter the kingdom of Heaven' (Matthew 18.2–3).

Try to set limits to the perceived disruption: indicate that, though once a month the service will be fairly lively, the Eucharist will be coherent and prayerful, and that adults and children alike will hear the Christian message.

Pre-empt obvious flash points. In one parish, there was a shudder of distaste when people saw the ominous words 'clapping Gloria' on the service sheet, but the priest adroitly pointed out that the refrain 'Gloria in excelsis Deo' was utterly traditional *and* we were smuggling a useful Latin phrase into the kids' liturgical vocabulary. Also, nobody could help noticing that the toddlers loved it.

It's almost impossible to advertise these services without using the word 'family' or 'children'. This encourages parents with young children (who may be nervous about coming into a church at all), and it's a clear indication that the noise levels will be up, but it can have the unintended effect of apparently excluding single, aged or gay parishioners.[5] Nothing but personal communication can really sort this, and a commitment to be completely inclusive in your engagement with the congregation.

Riots

These don't happen, but the chance of things getting out of hand is on everyone's mind. Whenever I talk to people about children's ministry one of the first things they ask is: 'How do you stop the children misbehaving?' Decide on a strategy for dealing with tricky children before the service. Large competent parents are a boon – the type who can just loom up and sit among them. If a child is irrepressible, giving her something to do or – better still – hold, normally calms her down. (This works with adults too.)

---

5 See page 27 for a sermon on the way Jesus calls us out of nuclear families to join the family of the Church.

Insist that the children put their hands up if they want to say something. This means you can react to a cheeky kid by saying, 'Yep, I can hear you, Tracey, put your hand up', while passing over the comment. There is *nothing* you can do about the child who comes up with a devastating put-down ('You're just making this up …') except be grateful that you're the one with the mike.

The only time the kids are likely to be over-excited will be after a session that they've found very funny, like a lesson on sheep stealing.

Mood Change

Build in a change a mood to finish the session. So, for example, you could ask a child to bring over the much stolen sheep. Talk to the sheep. 'Poor Sean, he doesn't know what's happening – are you OK, mate?' Crumple the sheep. 'Look at that – he's fed up …' (to a child) 'would you look after him for me?'

One way of dealing with a bunch of very lively kids is to give them something loud to do. It won't get out of hand if you stay in charge of the cues and have the exit line ready. So after the sermon on the first Sunday of Advent, you can entrust the children to give the Advent admonition to the church (see page 5).

You will be able to gauge the sermons and activities that are likely to create a buzz. Release it by having a swinging hymn ready to finish a panto, or simply encourage a round of applause.

Noise

Keep half an ear tuned in to the background noise. The pleasant burble of babies and toddlers is not a problem, though wailing babies may be – but encouraging their parents to walk them up and down, or attending to their needs in an adjoining room, usually sorts it. If small kids (aged four and upwards) start talking, it probably means they're bored; and a gradual rise in coughs, wriggles and things being dropped on the floor means you've definitely lost their attention. If things look desperate, wrap it up ...[6]

> ### Noise
> One gets the feeling that Our Lord wasn't too bothered by noise. We read of many people in the Gospels who yell to attract His attention: He always responds (*Matthew 15.21–28; Matthew 20.29–34; Mark 10.46–52*).

Grown-up chat is unacceptable – clock it up and work out when it comes. In some churches there can be a buzz of talk at the reception of Communion, a well-placed hymn often stops it.

Don't worry if you are not surrounded by big smiles, children don't necessarily smile when they are absorbed, they often look serious. Utter silence during a sermon is a huge compliment.

---

[6] A trusted colleague is invaluable if you're worried about audience reaction. Somebody who can say after the service, 'You were doing well until you drifted off on to ...' – whatever.

Performing

Know the space

There is nothing like knowing your performing space.

> In the Gospels we see Jesus adapting to the setting in which he finds Himself before He preaches:
>
> Again He began to teach beside the lake. Such a very large crowd gathered around Him that He got into a boat on the lake and sat there, while the whole crowd was beside the lake on the land. (*Mark 4.1*).
>
> When Jesus saw the crowds, He went up the mountain; and after He sat down, His disciples came to Him. Then He began to speak ... (*Matthew 5.1–2*).

Pace round the front end of your church. How much room is there? Are there any levels? A ledge, some useful sanctuary steps, a platform of any sort: a sermon that involves drama will benefit immensely from these things. (Angels, for example, look good appearing from a height – if you haven't got a step, put them in the pulpit.)

Think through the exits and entrances: if the three Kings appear halfway through your sermon – see page 37 – set them up to come up from the back of the church. If you and the children are going to follow Jesus as He goes round Galilee, weave round the church – people on the side aisles love a surprise appearance from the sanctuary party. A sudden posse of armed knights can be hidden behind the hymn books ...

LX and FX

Is the area well lit? Where are the power points, can you change the lighting state? It always looks good if you are able to put somebody on LX (shorthand for 'electrics') duty – say, 'OK, Jim, LX state 2' and the lights dim or brighten apparently by magic. FX ('effects') are even more exciting, though bear in mind that small children are frightened by loud noises.

However, everyone likes a ripple of bells, or the keyboard player swinging into the *Star Wars* theme when angels or spacemen enter.

Sound

Check the sound beforehand. *Always* carry batteries, and safety pins (to attach a lapel mike that's lost its clip). If you are visiting another church, investigate the sound set-up. A fixed mike ties you to the spot, a roving mike uses up one hand, mikes that get clamped to your head knock off your glasses – so, supposing you have a choice, go for a lapel mike. Discover if there is someone in control at a sound desk and try to get rid of them – at least as far as you are concerned. You must be in control of your own mike, otherwise you can't ad lib. (You can sometimes mollify the techie by putting him/her in charge of the music. Audio clips come across much better if they are faded in and out on cue.)

Good sound and lighting 'dress' a performance and make a huge difference. If you are going to throw any money at your family services, then spend it on sound, any extra can go on a good spotlight.

Budget

There never seems to be an obvious moment to talk about money, but decent kit suggests a budget. Setting a budget will a) indicate the importance your church attaches to family services, and b) put it on the PCC agenda. There is nothing like talking money for PCC members to start taking children's ministry seriously.

Hi-tech extras

Slide projection in church is almost as divisive as hand clapping. If you do happen to use one for hymn numbers, turn it off for the sermon. Sometimes an overhead projector can be useful for some swift drawing on transparencies, but the beam usually hits the preacher in the face and a lit blank screen is distracting. The church is more akin to theatre than cinema from a performer's point of view, and (unfortunately) a modern audience is more likely to watch a screen than a live performance. Don't give them the chance! Nothing gets a message across better than a real person, holding a show together, centre stage.

Tablets and mobile phones on the other hand are increasingly useful. You can apparently call up the Pope, or get a text from St Paul mid-address, you can produce instant FX – a thunderstorm perhaps, or the sound of the Tardis – and if you are stuck with having to read bits of your address, the text on a tablet is visible in a candlelit church – *and* lights up your face. As a last resort you can even access the internet. One Epiphany we needed a chalk blessing in a hurry (see page 39) and a genius server came to our rescue with a prayer she'd called up on her mobile.

Low-tech

There's a lot to be said for low-tech. Outside the church everyone does high-tech very well. We're good at candlelight, atmosphere and timelessness. (Some of this is discussed below.) From a sermon point of view, DIY props are totally disarming. Embrace cardboard boxes and string – children are delighted with wrapping paper and swiftly drawn pictures. The scripts assume you can lay your hands on an A1 flip-chart and an endless supply of Blu Tack and ping pong balls.

Scenery

Look at the iconography round you – is there anything you can draw attention to in the sermon? – 'We have the Holy Lamb Himself above the altar', 'Look, there's a picture of St Peter, can you see what he's got in his hand?', 'Somebody has painted JHS all over the walls …' (The latter works very well in a sermon on the Holy Name; kids like the puzzle involved in working out the initials.) The most modern stripped pine church usually has something, even if it's only a chalice and a bunch of grapes on the altar frontal.

Be up-beat about everything. All you need to know is what you've got. If you're surrounded by nothing but wood panelling, well one day you can give a sermon *on* wood – Noah building his ark, the oak at Mamre, Jesus and Joseph as carpenters and, supremely, the wood of the Cross. Even a concrete bunker church may suggest the sepulchre, or a story about a 'strong fortress is our God'.[7]

The performance space may be all too familiar to you, but walk round it beforehand. Each sermon will demand a slightly different configuration, and you may need to accommodate a seasonal obstruction – like the Paschal Candle or the Harvest display.

Check your props

It's obvious – but they need to be at hand, and in the right order. A server or child will probably be delighted to help out as prop manager.

Centre stage

You're the preacher, the one with the mike. The very word 'sermon' gives you a huge advantage; everyone is expecting to listen to you. Don't be apologetic – no 'Would you mind if …' or 'Would you like to …?' Call the kids to the front. Get them seated – 'Nope, nearer than that, great, now I can see you!'

Eyeball your audience: look at the kids you're talking to, look up and engage the rest of the congregation, give any other performer your undivided attention. If you do look at the audience while somebody else is speaking, it's only to give an implicit 'She's good, isn't she?'

> Jesus was clearly the natural centre of the synagogue when He preached:
>
> When He came to Nazareth, where He had been brought up, He went to the synagogue on the sabbath day, as was His custom. He stood up to read, and the scroll of the prophet Isaiah was given to Him … And He rolled up the scroll, gave it back to the attendant, and sat down. The eyes of all in the synagogue were fixed on Him. Then He began to say to them, 'Today this scripture has been fulfilled in your hearing.' (*Luke 4.16-17, 20–21*).

---

7 While writing this book I was asked to talk at an All Age service at a church I didn't know and arrived late. There was no time to take on board the richness of the decoration, so I missed a trick. The Old Testament passage was about Abraham being told to look at the stars in the sky and, if I'd only known, I could have asked the kids to look up at the ceiling – it was covered with stars …

28 General Principles

The liturgical setting

The sermons below are informal, but they sit easily in a formal service, in fact they draw on the setting and materials of a Eucharist. In particular, they lend themselves to the use of the ceremonies, sounds and smells of the catholic tradition. Obviously you will adapt them to your own churchmanship, but consider some extras – most kids get a thrill out of dinging bells, joining processions, or watching a priest get into her clobber …

The section below assumes the family service is a Eucharist; many of the suggestions offered can be adapted to non-eucharistic worship, but they work best in the context of a traditional Mass.

Family Eucharist/Mass

An obvious place for older children in a Family Mass is at the altar. Any child can hold a candle or ring a bell. If you haven't got a junior serving team, consider starting one, though not one exclusively made up of kids. Boys especially like serving with grown men, and being a teenage server is practically a vocation in itself. A cool dude acts as a role model for his smaller colleagues, and demonstrates to the kids in the pews that church is not just for mums and dads.

If you haven't got the resources for a full-blown serving team, you'll find there are many ways in which children (and adults) can actively participate in the Eucharist. Let's start with music.

Music for children

Anglicans are blessed with a fine tradition of hymns and sacred music. The sort of music you sing will depend on your resources, but it's a good idea to establish a core repertory. Choose one setting for the chants ('Lord have mercy'/the Gloria/'Holy Holy Holy'/'Blessed is He'/'Lamb of God') and stick to it. The congregation normally picks up the tune after a couple of services, and familiar chants help to bolt the service together. There are several cheerful Mass settings available: an easily learnt one is *A New People's Mass* by A. Gregory Murray.

Consider setting up a junior choir. It's a great way to involve the children, especially if they follow the programme devised by the Royal School of Church Music (RSCM); this rewards choristers with a series of medals for being on time, attending to the service, not wriggling, and learning to sing. It also attracts a certain sort of parent – musical, ambitious, a little pushy perhaps – who (we've discovered) wouldn't dream of coming to a service normally, but will turn up anywhere to hear their child sing.

Hymns

Hymn references in this book invariably direct the reader to a printed source (usually the *New English Hymnal* or the *Celebration Hymnal*) and not to the internet. The latter is an excellent source for locating hymns but, as its texts are usually taken from American hymn books, downloading them may result in your congregation being deprived of some well-loved English idioms. (The online 'Good King Wenceslas' or the last verse of 'Jerusalem the Golden' are cases in point …)

Liturgical and biblical texts

The scripts are based on the liturgies provided by *Common Worship* and, in some cases, *The Book of Common Prayer*. Psalm texts come from a variety of sources, as do quotes from the Bible. Young Anglicans are the fortunate inheritors of a wide range of Bible translations and I have used as many as possible – sometimes going for the plainest of modern translations (which I take to be the Good News Bible), or the Revised Standard Version, the New Revised Standard Version and, on occasion, some historic verses from the Authorized Version. Other liturgies and translations have inevitably piled up, chief among which are the Sunday Missal and the New Jerusalem Study Bible.

Setting up a Family Eucharist

Setting Up

Look round for the kids who have turned up early and scoop them up. Most kids like being given jobs – helping with the set-up identifies them as members of the church, and creates a pleasant buzz. They can:

- Help the welcome team by handing out service sheets and hymn books. Anchor the little ones to their parents for this job; small children love handing over hymn books, but they are agonizingly slow. From seven up, children are extremely efficient.
- Assist you in preparing the church for worship: set the Gospel book on the altar (unless it's brought in by procession at the start of the service).

- Light the candles,[8] place the collection plates and/or the bread and wine that will be brought up in the Offertory.
- Make the front pews look attractive with tidy kneelers and booklets.
- Arrange mats for the other kids to sit on down the front.
- Sort out a buggy park.

---

[8] This book assumes that you follow your church's Health and Safety guidelines in all procedures involving children.

- Sitting in the front pews is an important part of ministry for worshippers, children and families. Their confident response to the service – kneeling, standing, crossing themselves – will be observed and imitated by newcomers. And you can rely on them in an emergency – to catch toddlers, share hymn books, and so on.

You can also:

- Give a child a specific job in the address, 'Would you mind being a pirate? Here's the hat …' Reassure them that it will be perfectly obvious when they are on and what they are to do.
- Give competent kids some glamorous tasks, like testing the mike, or preparing the prop table.

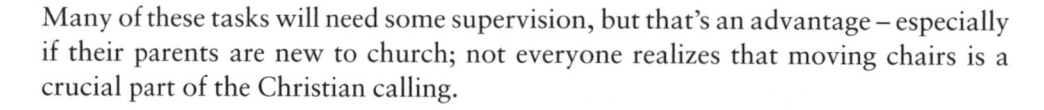

Many of these tasks will need some supervision, but that's an advantage – especially if their parents are new to church; not everyone realizes that moving chairs is a crucial part of the Christian calling.

Getting the Team Together

All performances go better for someone to bounce off. A comedian often bounces off the audience – and the kids will be delighted to let you do that – but you'll find things go 100 per cent better if you have another performer up there with you. Somebody you can guarantee to give the scripted response and pick up a cue. (This is not the moment to recruit 'nice but dim Tim' – be ruthless, find a natural. It could be a teenager.) This person is your 'straight man', 'stooge' and sometimes, if you are doing a double-hander, 'Preacher 2' (see Scripts 15 and 29). You will also find that, if two of you run through the scripts beforehand, you won't get double the ideas – but *ten* times more than if you were thrashing it out by yourself.

Stage and Prop Managers

Gather reliable people to help as stage crew and techies. One person prepared to hold a map upside down will free up your hands, and give you somebody with whom to share the joke.

Have the props to hand. Children make good prop managers – but don't reveal the prop table too early as they usually can't resist fiddling with them.

If you are using pictures provided on the Hymns Ancient and Modern website, at www.canterburypress.co.uk/downloads, have an A1 flip-chart ready. (Any smaller and it won't be seen.) Recruit someone to stick the pictures up – it means you won't get tangled up in magic tape, and it's sometimes fatal to turn your back on a bunch of kids …

Supporting Cast

Ask everyone in the sanctuary or on the serving team to look, listen and react throughout the address – especially if they are in the eye-line of the congregation.

In church, as in the theatre, the congregation immediately spots the person who is not involved. If you think the younger servers are going to wriggle throughout, put them in the audience. You're ready to go ...

Taking Command

Be completely confident about the service you are about to offer. It is the central act of worship of the Church and utterly trustworthy in theology, prayer, reading and action. Moreover, it has an immediate appeal for children. Mercifully, Jesus didn't tell His disciples to turn to page 142 in the service book, He said, '*Do* this ...' (In fact, this is one of the few things He actually *did* command us to do.) And what He did was to take bread, bless it, break it, and give it to His friends. Those four actions have been performed whenever Christians have gathered to obey Our Lord's command, and their physicality, their very ordinariness, have created a whole range of personal gesture and liturgical action deemed fitting – and useful – to involve everybody in the great drama of the Mass.

Doing Things

Many of these gestures can be offered to children at once. They may not have the words to express their feelings as they approach Jesus at the altar (nor, come to think of it, do many adults) but they can all bend the knee ...

And the knee, remembering the dip and recovery to the upright, sets off a muscular memory which reinforces and, to some extent, supplies the devotion they are trying to feel. The gesture is in fact a prayer.

In short, an ordinary Eucharist for families and/or large numbers of children is an extremely effective act of worship, especially when celebrated with solemnity.[9] In what follows, the service will be described with a liturgically rich setting in mind, leaving it to individual readers and churches to adapt it to their own churchmanship and resources.

Performance

The Mass hinges on action, and people in the sanctuary need to be on the ball if they are to engage the congregation. People can read body language with devastating accuracy and will know at once as a priest or deacon holds up the Gospel book whether they believe in what they are doing.

Not holding up the Gospel, and shoving it under your seat when you have finished, is as telling an action as enthroning it at the end of the reading. Perhaps you *may* want to indicate that God's Word is more important than the volume in which it is housed. That's fine, as long as you are conscious what signals your physical gestures are sending out. All services happen in physical space: they have actions, props, entrances and exits, and the main playing area has to have space, light and sound.

Wardrobe

The Eucharist typically comes with costumes: venerable, colourful – and useful.

Priests

Traditional vestments identify the key performers at the altar and, curiously, render them anonymous.

---

9 Solemnity in the old-fashioned sense of *ceremonious* or *seemly*: this doesn't preclude being cheerful ...

36 Setting up a Family Eucharist

As you encumber yourself with a cope, or a bright green chasuble, this might not seem particularly obvious, but it works. A robed priest is just that – a robed priest, not Father Kevin or Mother Melanie. Standing at the altar the people see a priest offering the Eucharist the way it has been offered since at least the third century. Priest and people enter a timeless world together. That sense of timelessness is one of the great strengths of a Mass. The liturgy is both remote (in fact, rather odd in places) and immediate: performed right now, reaching back to the Early Church, and part of the eternal worship of Heaven. A sense of the holy, of the numinous, is something anyone can respond to – children, toddlers, even wary adults.

And of course wearing ancient garments is both fun and interesting. There is a session on the meaning of the components of the traditional dress of priest and deacon on pages 116–22. (This is a useful session to introduce a new curate to the church.) And, once the congregation get used to vestments, they start to enjoy the variations – the change from green to purple at the start of Lent, or the addition of some Cinderella props during the Christmas sermon.

Casting the curate as the villain or …   *Cinderella, always goes down well*

Servers

Once you've decided on the priest's kit, cast an eye on the servers. Most kids under 12 don't mind dressing up and it's worth investing in some extra albs, or traditional cassocks and cottas.

School shoes (black) look neat with a black cassock, though many kids feel that trainers give a certain street cred to the sanctuary. Church isn't school, and personally I'd let them flash their cool footwear.

Props

A family service is the time to bring out your props. Essential props for a Eucharist using a young serving team are at least two candles in holders, and a sanctuary bell – if you haven't got one, buy a small hand bell with a sweet tone (not a massive great playground bell). You'll also need a glass bowl and glass jug, small enough for a child to handle, and a small processional cross if you intend to have a child crucifer.

Then of course there are the ordinary flasks for the wine and water, the ciborium (vessel for the wafers) and the napkins on the credence table. Setting up the altar gives your serving party some interesting things to do, and fascinates the kids in the pews.

Less is more however: the kids' attention is caught only if they are allowed to approach the altar every now and then. And an explicit commentary on what is happening – a Teaching Mass as it's called – is more effective if it is only done once a year.

Bringing the water to the altar ... and watching the lavabo

One of the reasons to use bells, candles and liturgical action is to make the Eucharist a habit and help people ease into the flow of the service. Not everything needs to be explained, light and gesture has its own meaning and, as worshippers get used to the pattern of the liturgy, they find that the sound of the bells, or the chink of a thurible chain, recalls them to devotion, even if they happen to be stuck behind a pillar. All the actions of Mass have a reason and I remember hearing a confirmation group using their knowledge of the service to evaluate the significance of the various portions of Scripture they heard each Sunday. 'The Gospel must be the most important' said one child. 'Why?' 'Because it's read from the *middle* of the church ...' This is not perhaps the most complete answer to the centrality of the Proclamation of the Gospel, but it's not a bad place to start.

I have left the most exciting prop to the end, the thurible ...

Incense

This book assumes that you can, when you wish, rustle up a thurible (an incense bowl on a chain) and a person to swing it, the thurifer.

Incense disappeared in Anglican parishes (more or less) after the Reformation[10] and, more recently, Vatican II ruled that, though it could be used at all celebrations of the Eucharist, it was not always necessary. This had the unintended effect of making incense an optional extra in Roman Catholic churches, and its habitual

---

10 Though bowls of incense were burned in Ely cathedral as late as the eighteenth century.

use in the Church of England is now confined to traditional Anglo-catholic services. I think that's a pity. The smell and the slight haze it produces flags up the holiness of the sanctuary and, long before it became a party badge among Christians, incense was one of the pleasantest (and blessedly unbloody) sacrifices of the Old Testament. The book of Revelation indicates that incense is used in Heaven, and to this day the Eastern churches use it as a continuous prayer throughout the Eucharist – not surprisingly, as it *is* a prayer in itself.[11]

Smoke

Incense may need getting used to, but it's worth noting that nobody is overcome with paroxysms of coughing unless they're standing right in the smoke and breathing deeply. (And not even then, young servers appear to imbibe smoke quite naturally).

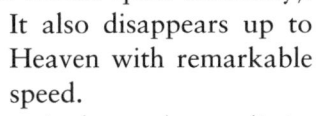

It also disappears up to Heaven with remarkable speed.

And, to be realistic, incense is a great way to keep your serving team together. Kids love the way the top of the thurible runs up and down its chain, they hover round as the charcoal is lit, and are deeply impressed by the priest's blessing of the incense grains, 'Be blessed by Him in whose honour you shall be burned.'

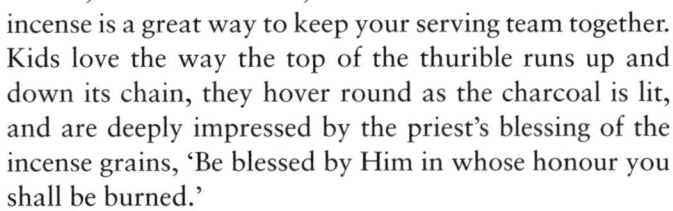

Incense means that you always have a job for the smallest child in the team – the boat boy/girl – and the job of thurifer is something the others can aspire to.

---

[11] 'And another angel came and stood at the altar with a golden censer ... and the smoke of the incense rose with the prayers of the saints from the hand of the angel before God.' (Revelation 8.3a, 4).

Extras

Liturgical extras are things often called 'sacramentals', offshoots of the sacraments – like holy water. Some churches provide a jug of holy water for people to fill up water bottles from and take home to bless their homes.

Then there are decorative extras, the lovely things we fill our churches with: Christmas trees, harvest sheaves, vegetable marrows and so on – stuff that has nothing to do with the actual service. Incense, bells and vestments, however, are *not* extras; they are so normal that they should slot into the service as an integral part of the liturgy.

Adapting the Mass for Children

Obviously a Family Mass is streamlined. As we go through the order of Mass below, you will notice that I go for many of the possible cuts and opt for any variation that can include children.

The Eucharist Step by Step

Entrance

The simplest Mass has to start somehow. The priest and servers have to get to the sanctuary, and on a Sunday they come in procession. Young altar servers enjoy the march round the church, and babies and toddlers are normally rendered speechless at the sight. One small boy at St Michael's used to watch the procession go by from one end of the pew, slide along to the other end – and catch it up as it turned the corner.

The procession is accompanied by an opening hymn and, traditionally, the congregation bow their heads as the processional cross passes, and again as the presiding priest brings up the rear. In both cases they are acknowledging Jesus, represented on the cross and by His servant, the priest. If you alert the children to watch out for the cross and Celebrant, you'll find they perform a sort of liturgical Mexican Wave as the procession goes by.

The priest and servers arrive at the altar and the celebrant starts the service with …

The Sign of the Cross

This gesture is a prayer and one the children can take away with them to use whenever they wish to ask for God's blessing – before meals, when they go to bed, or if they want to get in touch with Him and can't think what to say.

It's here that family services come into their own. Congregations who do not usually cross themselves are not too bothered if the kids are taught to do so, and usually fascinated to hear the reason for the action. Naturally you can't highlight everything you do, but on some Sundays – Holy Cross Day for example – this bit of the Mass could receive special attention.

One way of leading the children in the Sign is:

We meet in the Name of the Father, who lives in Heaven
1 *Touch the head*
And of the Son, who came down to Earth
2 *Bring hand down to tummy*
And of the Spirit, who lives in our hearts
3 *Touch the left side of the chest*
Amen
4 *Touch the right side of the chest*

The Sign for small children

Small children simply need to know the shape of a cross, and very little ones can be encouraged to *be* crosses. Show them how by standing tall and spreading out your arms, congratulate them when they have done this with an 'Amen!'

Or you can teach them the action without the trinitarian prayer. Ask the kids to move their hand from head to tum, shoulder to shoulder, as they say:

1) I
2) love
3) you
4) Lord
Amen

Or some Sundays you can brisk things up and get the kids to make the biggest cross they can manage by saying:

Priest: Prayer is really simple. Sometimes we pray by making a huge cross in the air. Can you do that? *Make a huge cross in the air with the children. Finish with an* **Amen**

The Sign of the Cross is a clear signal that the service has begun and gives you a precious couple of seconds to catch the children's attention. Use them to go straight into the next section.

The Greeting

The Sign of the Cross *is* a Greeting, and it's better not to hang about, packing in every last introductory sentence from *Common Worship*. That said, a Family Eucharist benefits from the priest welcoming the people, and indicating there's still room down the front. The informality of this moment gives you a chance to introduce the theme for the day. Limit this to one sentence, and move straight on to the Penitential Rite.

Penitential Rite/Kyrie

The Penitential Rite, placed as it is at the beginning of the service, gives everyone a chance to dump the failures and sins of the week at the foot of the Cross. There are various forms of general confession in *Common Worship,* but nothing beats the Kyrie. The children find its threefold structure satisfying and it is infinitely adaptable. When using the Kyrie as a confession, each petition is prefaced with a short sentence, directed to one of the Persons of the Trinity. It's a good pattern for family worship and the children appear to tick off the Holy Trinity as they go. One version could be:

Celebrant	Lord God our Father, you always forgive those who admit they are wrong
	Lord have mercy
People	**Lord have mercy**
Celebrant	Lord Jesus, we are sorry for the times we have been unloving and unthankful
	Christ have mercy
People	**Christ have mercy**
Celebrant	Lord the Holy Spirit, you show us how we should forgive others
	Lord have mercy
People	**Lord have mercy**

The General Confession

The beginning of a penitential season might be a good time to use a form of General Confession: this prayer, said soberly by the entire church, is an acknowledgement that, as sinners, we're all in the same boat. Of the two offered in *Common Worship* the first, the one that starts 'Almighty God, our heavenly Father' has the most straightforward words for a family service. A graphic gesture, indeed a prayer in itself, is to thump the chest at the words 'through our own deliberate fault'. Children find the action extremely impressive.

The Absolution

The Penitential Rite ends with an Absolution. The ✠ in the text indicates that, as the priest absolves the people, they respond tactilely by crossing themselves.

Celebrant	May Almighty God ✠ forgive you your sins and bring you to eternal life through Jesus Christ our Lord
People	Amen

Asperges

'Asperges' is Latin for 'sprinkling'. A popular way to end the Absolution is to sprinkle the children with holy water: the sheer fun of getting wet helps them feel the joy of forgiveness.

Asperges are normally performed with an aspergillum (holy water bowl) and a sprinkler, but an ordinary bowl and some twigs of rosemary make a good substitute.

In a family service the sprinkling can be prefaced with a sentence on holy water as a symbol of God's power to cleanse us from our sins, followed by a warning that everyone is about to get splashed. The priest starts by sprinkling himself/herself, by making the Sign of the Cross over their body with the sprinkler, then sprinkling the serving team. Ask the children to watch how the servers are sprinkled – they bow and cross themselves – and see if they can follow suit. The size of the congregation will determine whether you sprinkle from the sanctuary steps, or walk down the aisle. The idea is to get everyone – don't forget the choir.

The Gloria

The Gloria is sung on all Sundays outside Advent and Lent. The point about the Gloria is that it's upbeat. If the kids have been kneeling for the Kyrie, get them to jump up to sing – and give them a swinging tune. There is the excellent 'Clapping Gloria' by Michael Anderson, and the *New English Hymnal* version, number 363, is best sung to the vigorous *Camberwell*.

Collect

Having signed themselves with the cross, confessed their sins and sung God's praise, the Christian community is now ready to pray together. The priest leads them in an opening prayer, the Collect.

Every now and then it's a good idea to literally 'collect' the congregation together – the juvenile part at least – by asking them to stand round the priest and pray together as the priestly people of God. For this you may like to show the kids how the very early Christians prayed, standing up, with their hands raised in the 'orans' ('praying') position.

The priest says the prayer and the children add an emphatic 'Amen'.

Readings

The Liturgy of the Word begins in earnest with the first reading. Normally four biblical extracts are read (Old Testament, New Testament, Psalm and the Gospel) but not on a Family Sunday.

The cutting room floor

Take a view as to what your main story is and streamline the first three readings to fit – in fact, consider cutting a couple. (Some readings, those that follow a difficult line of argument, or warn their hearers against fornication and other adult sins, expunge themselves.)

Use the kids. The older ones can read – probably very well – and this is a great moment to include children who aren't interested in serving or singing. Use a modern version of the Bible, adjust the microphone for the size of the reader, and try to rehearse the child before the service.

The script

To help their delivery, it's useful to print out the reading beforehand in large font, with obvious line breaks and the rhetorical phrasing clearly marked.

So, *not* a chunk of text like this:

Elijah went into the wilderness and, sitting under a furze tree, he wished he was dead: 'Lord,' he said, 'it is enough. Take my life; I am no better than my ancestors.' Then he lay under the furze tree and fell asleep.

But:

Elijah went into the wilderness and,
sitting under a furze tree,
he wished he was dead.

'Lord,' he said, 'it is enough.
Take my life, I am no better than my ancestors!'

Then he lay under the furze tree and fell asleep.

Children have a slight tendency to rush. This sort of spacing slows them down – as does explaining to them that adults need time to register what they are saying. ('Grown-ups aren't as quick as you …') Small children may need a platform to stand on, and sometimes welcome the presence of a supportive grown-up.

If you can get a natural performer (often a teenager) to do one of the readings, free them from the lectern and let them engage the children just as they wish. Less is more as far as (apparent) casualness is concerned, but a relaxed performance of one of the readings can be a moment of light relief, and enhances the formal reading of the Gospel.

Gospel Procession

The Liturgy of the Word builds to a crescendo. It starts with the Jewish Scriptures, moves on to the New Testament, and ends with a passage from the Holy Gospel. To mark this the Gospel book is traditionally processed from the altar to be read among the people. It is preceded by incense and the cross, attended by candles, and held aloft by the person about to read it (ideally a deacon).

Children find this kind of ceremony very exciting, and for adults it's a marvellous moment of formality, and slight dottiness. The raising of the Gospel is a ceremonial acknowledgement that Christ is present in His Gospel, just as later He will be present in the sacrament of the altar.

The procession is apparently a Greek Orthodox idea – it's supposed to replicate the wandering of Jesus as He went preaching round Galilee. Whatever the reason, it works perfectly. The congregation stop acting like an audience, they stand up as the Gospel book passes them, and turn to face it. Most people in church can only see the cross, the smoke, and the formal raising of the Gospel at the beginning and end of the reading – but they can be in no doubt that Christ is in the midst of His people.

Gospel in the Middle

On some Sundays, and depending on numbers, you may invite the children to join the Gospel procession, either carrying candles in portable holders, or little battery-operated garden lights. This sort of variation only works if it is used sparingly. Most kids feel a thrill when they are at last allowed to join the serving team.

Before the Gospel is read it is censed, to remind us that God's word is holy, and the words are marked with the Sign of the Cross.

This is all so physical it is a good idea to get the children to join in. It is usual to make three little crosses on your body as the Gospel is announced – one on the forehead, one on the lips, and one on the chest – to remind us that the Gospel is to be understood, proclaimed and cherished.

After the Proclamation of the Gospel, the reader kisses the book, the procession re-forms, and the Gospel is 'enthroned' (usually on a lectern) and we're into the kids' sermon.

The change of gear is startling. One minute the Gospel is processed with majesty and holiness, the next it is unpacked by a relaxed preacher, with a box of tricks and some terrible jokes. The end result is that people register the Gospel as august, wonderful and utterly accessible, like the Eucharist itself.

Don't lose the plot ...

The homilies in this book are all based on the Gospel of the day. This means it's important that it's the last thing the congregation hears before the address begins. Try to avoid delays and insertions, such as songs or notices,[12] between the Gospel and the preacher: children will not necessarily link the two sections if their concentration is broken.

Variations

As with all formal structures, whether in church or theatre, the slightest variation in format has an enormous effect. You can only pull this trick a couple of times, but some of the scripts deliberately buck expectation by starting *before* the Gospel – leaving it for Jesus, in the Gospel passage, to deliver the punch line – while the Annunciation Gospel stops mid-track to accommodate the sudden appearance of an angel ... (page 55)

---

[12] Which begs the question as to where you *do* put the notices. After the Post Communion prayer and before the Blessing causes the least disruption.

Sermon

The sermon (or address) marks a gear change in the service; it is the moment when the Mass turns from word to action. The congregation move from being listeners to participants and, in a family service, the sermon can actually effect this change. The kids scamper down to the front, free up, and sent back to take part in the Liturgy of the Eucharist. A great deal hinges on the homily and, to pull it off, it helps to think of it as a mini-show.

Dynamics

Where, for example, are your audience? Down the front – especially if they are very small.

To get them there you either rope off the front pews for kids or, as some families prefer to sit together, call them to the front. Now, why would any child want to come forward? Well, partly your engaging personality – but also because there's something they can only see from the front of the church. A flip-chart is very helpful on these occasions. 'Perhaps the children would like to come down to the front and help Sarah with the pictures' is the normal invitation at St Michael's. The occasion when we said we were about to cut a lady in half provoked a stampede.

Once the children are down the front, give them opportunities to interact. It is the way they are taught in the classroom and modern children are not usually bothered about getting up in front of an audience. They can give you a hand with a picture, or show you how to use a transformer toy, or drop dead on command.

Numbers

Make a realistic assessment of how you can involve your audience. Up to 20 kids and you can ask them to help you draw things, or join in the story; over 20 and there will be too many disappointed would-be performers. However, large numbers of children can be used as a crowd, they can provide sound FX (see Script 10), or leap up and down on cue.

Of course, using kids as extras has its drawbacks. How do you get a flock of 50 sheep to stop bleating, for example? The answer is to rehearse sound FX as you go. Tell them what the noise is, cue it in with an obvious downbeat of your hand, then show them how to 'kill it'. Children love this phrase and the theatrical gesture that goes with it, drawing a finger emphatically across the throat. Practise this a couple of times, making sure – if they *are* sheep – that you cut the kids off mid baa.

Art

If you can draw at all, you are made – there is something about a picture appearing at the end of a pen that mesmerizes an audience – but there are lots of ways round this for the non-artistic. All the scripts in this book offer short-cuts for people who are nervy about drawing, or provide ready-made pictures that you can slap up as you tell a story. In whatever way you present the pictures, try to interact with them. Look at the villain as you stick him up and comment on his features, 'What do you think? Is he a nice guy or not?' ('NO!' from the kids.)

Variety performance

Every trick of the trade is possible in the sermon. The Mass is amazingly robust and can contain any activity whose ultimate goal is making the Gospel live. The revelation one Epiphany that all the kings' gifts included chocolate caused a sensation … (see Script 9)

But of course there's nothing like a straight story, especially if your sightlines – and knees – permit you to sit on the floor with the kids. Some of the stories below are illustrated with pictures that can be downloaded from www.canterbury press.co.uk/downloads; others use simple props, or call for some carefully scripted 'spontaneity'.

Stick to the script

All the scripts stick to the 'One Point per Sermon' rule. That's not supposed to inhibit you from throwing in gags, just don't throw in another Impressive Moral. If the preacher is not one of the clergy, ask him or her to run any extra business past a priest before they deliver the address. The scripts are completely orthodox and, though the vicar is not likely to slide into heresy, it is astonishing how often a well-meaning volunteer does.

Winding it up

Finishing a sermon is notoriously hard. A children's homily has to get the kids back to their seats, and provide the jump-off point for the rest of the service. Various exits are offered in the scripts.

Who are the sermons for?

Sermons, like the Epiphany one described above, are intended for All Age worship – which raises the question, 'How All Age are they?' They appear to address the kids, but are intended for the whole congregation. We have found that you can teach a great deal more doctrine than is commonly thought in a family service; it nourishes the adults,[13] and everyone benefits from the simple accessible language. Children are naturally speculative and interested in metaphysics and, given a clear presentation, will be able to follow you as you consider the implications of Jesus' Ascension, the timelessness of God, or the dual nature of Christ. The Old Lags in the congregation are often heartaningly enthused by the sermon, from them you can expect remarks like, 'I never knew that's what the "Proper" was ...'

---

13 There is no way of knowing if these addresses engage teenagers, but the same could be said of practically any sermon, including those used in a Youth Mass. Many adolescents would die rather than react, it's something we have to live with.

Creed

The Eucharist continues with the Creed. It is always said at the principal Mass on a Sunday, and is something the kids can be encouraged to learn by heart. The shortest of the three classic creeds, the Apostles', is the obvious one to use at a Family Mass – especially when split into the sequence of questions and answers found in the rite of Holy Baptism.

For small children, a short trinitarian creed can be found in *The Celebration Hymnal* 130, set to a folk tune adapted by Vaughan Williams (just use verse 1). A clapping version of this goes down well:

I believe in God the Father	clap
I believe in God the Son	clap
I believe in God the Spirit,	clap
God the Three	3 claps
and God the One.	clap

Intercessions

The action of the Mass moves towards the altar as the prayers and gifts of the Church are gathered up to be offered to God, starting with our prayers.

Kids are good at praying and make excellent intercessors. If there's time, ask a couple of them to write the intercessions for you. They usually approach the job in a business-like way and are blessedly brief. Ask them to come up with a one-liner on the needs of the world, the nation, the community, the parish, and themselves (starting a new school, breaking for half term, anything that's on their minds). The only thing children need to be taught is to pause. Ask them to say 'Jesus' quietly to themselves, three times, between the petitions – that will give the rest of the church time to pray.

If there's no time for the children to write intercessions, ask them to follow a simple format provided by the priest – or use the intercessions provided in the Appendix: Children's Liturgy for Good Friday, page 151. Rehearsing the young intercessor pays dividends, though you will need a grown-up on hand if members of the parish, present or departed, are mentioned by name. (A kid stumbling over a surname might upset the family.)

The Peace

The Peace has always been an integral part of Mass, though for years people watched the altar party exchange a formal Kiss of Peace, while contenting themselves with a dutiful 'and with thy spirit' when the priest offered the Peace to them. All that changed in the 1960s when the bishops asked their flock to exchange a sign of Christ's peace with one another. This embarrassed everyone and there was a certain amount of tight-lipped 'peace be with you' in the pews but now, after 60 years of shaking hands with complete strangers, the Peace is one of the most popular bits of the service. The gusto with which young children offer the peace sends a wave of good fellowship throughout the church. The idea that we are one family suddenly seems feasible.

The Kiss of Peace

Normally the congregation shake hands with each other, but sometimes the children can be encouraged to exchange a ceremonial Kiss of Peace.[14]

This is done by the person giving the Peace placing his or her hands on the shoulders of the person receiving it and saying, 'Peace be with you'. The recipient places their hands under the elbows of the peace-giver and replies, 'and with thy spirit/and also with you'. The 'kiss' is like a continental greeting, the head moving to the right shoulder of the other person, then the left.

Children find the formality fascinating, and the Kiss goes well with any address that emphasizes the courtesy of God and His angels in their dealings with us. The altar party should always give each other a formal Peace: it's one of those slightly odd actions which emphasizes the otherworldly character of the sanctuary.

Offertory

Bringing up the bread and wine, and helping with the collection, is an obvious moment to enlist the children's help.

It's also an exciting moment for the junior servers, who can assist by handing over the elements, place the palls, and be on hand for the lavabo. You may like to invite kids from the congregation to cluster round the altar as you talk through what happens – though this gains from only being done occasionally. (It also adds ten minutes to the service.)

---

14 St Paul loved this greeting; he enjoined his fellow Christians three times at least to: 'Greet one another with a holy kiss' (1 Corinthians 16.20 2; Corinthians 13.12; and Romans 16.16).

Offertory processions can suffer from false starts; ask some adults to shepherd the kids up the aisle. Hand the gifts to the servers, bow, and retire.

Setting up the Altar

The children will understand what is happening much better if you let them handle the holy props. They can pass you the ciborium, the flasks of water and wine, and you may allow a sensible one to pour in a little water as you say the prayer, 'By the mystery of this water and wine …'

Ask a young server to hand you the palls, another to pour the lavabo, and have a small child ready with a purificator. Say the customary prayer and wash your hands. By this time the kids will be fascinated in everything – even the purificator.

Cense the gifts with no further commentary; it's time to let the rhythm of the Mass take over.

The Eucharistic Prayer

The climax of the Mass is attended by bells, lights, smoke and music as the Four Actions of Jesus at the Last Supper are faithfully replicated by the priest.

Eucharistic prayer H in *Common Worship* is very suitable for a Family Eucharist. It is provided in the Appendix: Eucharistic Prayer H, p. 149.

No commentary is possible during this great prayer, but many of the actions can be unpacked in a homily. The one on page 136 addresses the fundamental question (and indeed disappointment) that children are usually too polite to articulate. Why is this bit of Mass called a meal (or, worse, 'Jesus' party') when it so obviously isn't?

Opening Dialogue

You can teach the opening dialogue just before you say it – as long as you have a couple of kids who know the traditional responses, and another pair who are prepared to bounce back with the modern version (below). The session goes like this:

Priest We have got to the holiest part of the Mass, the Prayer of Consecration – and we start by having a conversation.

Run through the opening dialogue – Eucharistic Prayer B is used throughout this section.

I'll begin, join in if you know the words.

Make sure a few do – the servers should be able to help you out

The Lord be with you.
And also with you.

Lift up your hearts.
We lift them to the Lord.

Let us give thanks to the Lord our God.
It is right to give thanks and praise.

This is one of the oldest bits of the Mass. The first bit is a greeting, the sort of things people used to say to each other back in Roman times; the second bit is *me* telling *you* to look up, and the third bit is *you* telling *me* it's OK to carry on.

Let's do that in modern English.

Good morning, kids!
Good morning, Father/Mother!

Look up, guys!
We *are* looking up.

How about us thanking God together?
OK, cool …

Got that? Let's do it together – but just before you do, can you *really* look up when I ask you to?

Practise that: get them to straighten up and look right up to Heaven

Excellent, there's nothing like straightening up as you pray, you feel fantastic.

Run the modern version again

Great – on the other hand, perhaps we ought to do the real version, it sounds politer.
Don't forget to look up though …

Run the traditional version

Brilliant, well, as you've given me permission to go on – I will …

Carry on with the rest of the prayer

The Preface

After the opening dialogue the priest appears to ad lib as a special thanksgiving, 'proper' to the season, is inserted. These are provided in *Common Worship*, but it is permissible to make one up on Sundays in ordinary time (when no particular festivity is being celebrated).

If there are only a few children round the altar, you can break off to ask them what they would like to thank God for this Sunday. It might be obvious – it's Epiphany, or Harvest, or half-term. Take what comes, agree that the fact that England is not doing too badly in the World Cup is a cause of great celebration, and (if you can think on your feet) make up a Preface thanking God for our games and the joy of running about. Even so, have a prepared Preface ready as a back-up and say it with the children.

Sanctus and Benedictus

These sections punctuate the Eucharistic Prayer and benefit from being sung.

A deep bow

Traditionally the sanctuary party bow low in the first part of the Sanctus. It's a good way to mark the holiness of this part of Mass and the children can be encouraged to join in.

Sympathize with the slight agitation many servers feel as to *when* to straighten up again. (It should be after the phrase 'God of power and might' or 'Lord God of hosts' depending on your translation.) See if the kids can get it right …

The Benedictus

The Sanctus is followed immediately by the Benedictus:

✠ Blessed is He that comes in the name of the Lord. Hosanna in the highest!

It is customary to make the Sign of the Cross as you say 'Blessed'.[15] The Benedictus and Sanctus can be run as one musical session in which the children learn the music for both – and bow/cross themselves on cue. After the Benedictus a child rings the sanctuary bell. This is the holiest part of the Mass: everyone kneels.

The Consecration

The church is usually perfectly still and focused as the priest repeats Jesus' actions at the Last Supper. This is the climax of the service and it is possible to involve children at the very centre of the action. As the Host and the Chalice are elevated, the serving party raise their candles, ring the bell three times, and the thurifer censes the Bread and Wine.

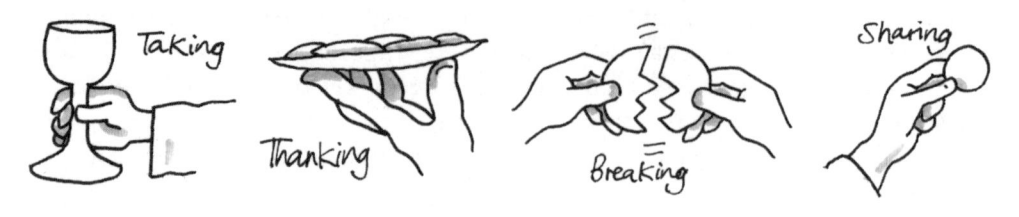

---

15 I asked a liturgically clued-up colleague why we did that once, he replied, 'because we're Anglican …' And there you have it. No reason *not* to do it though …

All these actions can be done by the children and teenagers in the serving team, and once in a while you may supplement them with extra candle holders and kids with small hand bells. You will need a senior server to cue them in, however – somebody who won't be exasperated by a very small kid dinging their bell inappropriately.

From the moment the Bread and Wine are consecrated nobody approaches the altar without genuflecting. Children pick up the distinction between a bow, a mark of respect, and a genuflection, a gesture of adoration (offered to Jesus, present in the Sacrament) very quickly.

Our Father

Consider using a musical setting of the Lord's Prayer. One can no longer guarantee that children know this prayer by heart and singing may help them memorize it.

Agnus Dei

This should be sung to an invariable tune.[16]

Holy Communion

Make sure the children come up for a blessing when Communion is being distributed. And, as this aspect can be a little hurried, encourage the celebrant to spend the time necessary for blessing each child individually. They find being able to feel the Sign of the Cross being marked on their heads very satisfying.

---

16 There is a sermon on Jesus as the Lamb of God in *Creative Ideas for Children's Worship: Year A*, Script 8 (Canterbury Press, 2011).

(Washing Up)

This is no part of Mass at all, just a sensible bit of tidying up. However, junior servers treat it very seriously, especially if they see adults disappear off to a side chapel and to do mysterious things with chalices. It's kind to let them help sometimes.

Wrapping it up

The end of Mass is deliberately brief. Having received Jesus in the sacrament, or received His blessing at the altar, it's time to go – to get out into the world and spread the Good News. The priest is usually extremely upbeat as he or she leads the Post Communion prayer and blesses the congregation.

Blessing

The Blessing is the last time the children perform a liturgical action. Preface the Blessing with 'Bow your heads and pray for God's Blessing ...' and encourage the kids to bow, and cross themselves, as you bless them in the name of the Trinity.

Dismissal

The traditional words 'The Mass is ended, go in peace to love and serve the Lord' indicates that it's over. Nothing more to do but go out to a swinging processional hymn and proclaim the gospel. The natural finishing point for a Mass is out on the street ...

But if there is a celebration in the church hall, an event in the church garden, or any extra activity that is happening in a safe and enclosed space, send the kids scampering off first, in the Name of Christ, as the final hymn breaks out.

The End Result

You can run a service like this without losing any of the majesty and prayerfulness of a normal Mass – as long as it is performed with utter confidence.

Success

As your team grows, you'll need to find things for the kids to do. Fortunately, that is rarely a problem. Along with the more normal functions of holding candles, or helping set up the altar, you can ask children to:

- Ring the small hand bell that signals various bits of the service.
- Hold up the service book for the priest, or be a living lectern for the Gospel.
- Take over the lavabo.
- Collect the reserved Sacrament, or be the kid who rings the bell as it is moved from the Tabernacle to the Altar.
- Ring the hand bell if the Sacrament is being taken to a pew-bound communicant.
- Help with the washing-up.
- Hold the incense boat. Being the boat boy/girl is the easiest way to occupy the smallest member of the team.
- Give a hand at busy moments with egg rolling at Easter, or receiving the gifts at Harvest.

Ready to go

The simplest way to introduce children and newcomers to the Eucharist is to do it, and a Family Mass – following the rubrics of *Common Worship* – can be found, laid out in booklet form, with illustrations at www.canterburypress.co.uk/downloads. You are very welcome to download this to use as a template for your own service booklet.

Rewards

Some of the scripts come with suggestions about little gifts you can hand out at the end of Mass: sweets, tiny devotional aids – even bits of fish-shaped pitta bread don't go amiss. But the major reward turns out to be what we all get from involving children in a service. The basic instruction (catechesis) one can slip into the sermon is often as useful for adults as children – and anyone who works with kids discovers very quickly they are holy, insightful and excellent metaphysicians.

Children's Addresses in a Non-eucharistic Service

It is perfectly possible to run a Liturgy of the Word for children without going on to the Liturgy of the Eucharist. In this case, the sermon is the climax of the service, though you may go on to include some prayers (particularly the Lord's Prayer), the Peace and a final hymn.

More informal services depend on your venue – a church hall, a leisure centre – the provision of sockets, and a rock band.[17] This sort of service frees you up for games[18] and extremely active worship songs, but the Proclamation of the Gospel, and its attendant address, draws the service together and – if you follow the lectionary readings – anchors your worship in the liturgy of the universal Church.

Sermons

Scripts for the major feasts and seasons of the Church's year are given below. In some cases two or three sermons are offered for the same day – on the assumption that, though you may not always celebrate Pentecost with a family service, you are practically bound to have one on Christmas Day or Easter Sunday.

The sermons assume you are following the lectionary; the Gospel may be cut, or slightly dramatized, but it is always the one for the day. Some Gospels are invariable, whatever lectionary year you are in (Epiphany, for example); others change with the year. The scripts for Advent, Christmas, Easter, and so on work with any of these variations.

> Jesus said, 'Let the little children come to me, and do not stop them; for it is to such as these that the kingdom of Heaven belongs' (*Matthew 19.14*).

---

17 In some civic centres there may be a ban on candles, and incense will almost certainly trigger the fire alarm.

18 Ideas for games and activities can be found in *Creative Ideas for Children's Worship*, for lectionary years A, B and C.

Script 1   Advent Sunday
(Advent Gospels)

(A) Matthew 24.42–44
(B) Mark 13.32–37
(C) Luke 21.25–26, 36

> **BEGINNINGS**
>
> Advent marks the beginning of the church year with a wake-up call. You can do this whole session with the script in one hand, but – as the situations are extremely obvious – you'll probably find it just as easy to ad lib; the important thing is to keep it moving.

SET UP

- A grown-up or teenager prepared to read through the script beforehand and be your stooge.
- A chair and a wallet.
- The bell to use for the Elevation and a server ready to ring it on cue.
- As the address highlights the Elevation, it benefits from being given by the Celebrant.[19]

ADDRESS

After the Gospel, ask the children to come to the front

>>OK, today we're going to talk about beginnings.
>>Does anyone know how we begin a race?
>>**(Ready, Steady, Go!)**
>>Can you show me?

Set the kids up to race down the aisle (or some of them! Take a view on the number of children present)

---

19 This is the elevation of the bread and wine after the words of institution. Not all priests hold up each element after it has been consecrated, but it would be useful to do so today.

Ready, Steady – Go!

Once they've got to the back

Did everyone get that? Let's do it again.
Ready, Steady – Go!

The kids race back

OK, let's try that some other ways.

Bang out the following commands; it doesn't matter what positions the children come up with

How about – Ready, Steady – JUMP!
Ready, Steady – DROP!
Ready, Steady – PRAY!

End with

Ready, Steady – SIT!
Brilliant – let's think what we're doing here.

(to the stooge)

Name, can you get into the 'READY POSITION'?

The stooge gets into an impossibly tense position

Hang on to that – I'm just going to get the Gospel book.

Wander off to get the book

Stooge	Oi!
Preacher	What?
Stooge	I can't stay like this –
Preacher	Why not?

Major wobble from the stooge

Stooge	Because I'm wobbling …
Preacher	Oh yes, sorry, I'll do the next bit – STEADY!

The stooge steadies himself

Preacher	OK, are you ready?
Stooge	Yup.
Preacher	And steady?
Stooge	Yes!
Preacher	*(Look at your watch)* Ah well, the race doesn't start for half an hour.

Exclamation from the stooge

Stooge	Well, I'm not going to stay like this for half an hour.

Sits down

Preacher	*(to the children)* And that's the problem. We can't be ready for ever. Jesus was very interested in people being ready, but He knew how difficult it was. In the Gospel today He tells us to be ready for – wait a minute, I'll look it up –

Refer to the Gospel

Yup, here it is. He wants us to be ready for –

Adapt this for whatever Gospel you have just read – the lead words are 'the Coming of the Son of Man' or 'the Master will return' or 'the Son of man will appear'. Look up to explain

Jesus is talking about the moment when He will come back to Earth. The trouble is, He doesn't tell us when that's going to be. He says it's like a bloke sitting up, making sure a burglar doesn't sneak in.

(To your stooge)

Could you do that?

Stooge	No problem!
Preacher	*(placing chair)* Oh yeah, well you sit there, and keep an eye on this.

Place your wallet in front of him

No nodding off.

Stooge	Certainly not!

The stooge ad libs as he/she settles down to watch the wallet

Yup, this is simple,
I'll keep an eye on this – *(yawn).*
Gosh, it's boring …

Nods off

Preacher	*(Do a double take)* Look at that! Asleep already! What would happen if a burglar crept in?

Encourage a couple of kids to creep up to steal the wallet. The stooge plays along with it; he/she almost wakes up (tell the kids to freeze when this happens), keep it snappy and, after an exciting couple of minutes, the wallet is stolen

Shake stooge

Oi! Where's my wallet?

4 Script 1 – Advent Sunday (Advent Gospels)

The stooge pulls a face or says 'Sorry, guv' or whatever seems suitable
To the children

> You see, it's very difficult to stay ready.
> Even so, Jesus wants us to be ready, watching out for the day He's going to come back.
> Now this is the first Sunday of Advent, the beginning of the new church year, and the message of Advent Sunday is …

Look in the Gospel again

> 'Wake up! Be ready!'
> That's obviously something we need to practise.
> One way to do it is to watch out for Jesus when He turns up in our church.
> He's everywhere.
> We can hear Him in the Bible …

Hand the Gospel book to the stooge

Stooge   *(riffling through)* Yup, this is all about Jesus.
Preacher   We can greet Him in our fellow Christians …

Shake hands with some kids

> But, best of all, we can recognize Him
> when I *(or name of priest)* hold Him up in the Bread at the Prayer of Consecration.
> Let's be ready for that.
> It's really easy,
> because *Name (bell ringing server)* will ring the bell three times when it happens – Can you show us that, *Name*?

Kid rings bell three times

> Fantastic. So when you hear that bell, look up, because Jesus Himself will be at our altar.
> And, just to finish, I think we should make sure the grown-ups remember the message of Advent.
> What is it?
> **(Wake up!)**
> *(Dubiously)* Ye-es, I don't think they'll hear that.
> **(WAKE UP!!)**
> That's more like it. Could you turn round?

To the congregation

	The children have got a message for you: OK, kids …
Children	**Wake up!**
Preacher	What do you think? They look very dozy to me – let's try again.
Children	**WAKE UP!!**
Preacher	Brilliant, thanks.

And on with the Eucharist – make sure the bell rings very emphatically at the Elevation.

Script 2 St John the Baptist

(A) Matthew 3.1–12 – cut to vs 1–6
(B) Mark 1.1–8 – cut to vs 4–8
(C) Luke 3.1–6 – cut to vs 2b–6

THEME

John the Baptist makes frequent appearances in the church year – on his feast days 24 June (birth) and 29 August (beheading), in Advent, and in the Christmas and Epiphany seasons when he baptizes Jesus, and hails Him as the Lamb of God. The sheer oddity of John's appearance and diet usually catches children's attention, which makes it easy – in Advent at least – to offer them a pithy resumé of his message.

SET UP

- A1 flip-chart and Pictures 2.1, 2.2a and 2.2b from www.canterburypress.co.uk/downloads.
- Kid prepared to play John the Baptist (girl or boy).
- Rucksack.
- Bottle of water.
- Bible.
- Jar of honey (stick a label on it, 'Wild Honey') and some grasshoppers (Picture 2.1). Hide them somewhere on the sanctuary steps for John to find.
- Set up another child or teenager to have his/her mobile stolen.

ADDRESS

> This Sunday we are thinking about a rather odd saint.
> His name was John.

Enter kid playing John

> John realized when he was fairly young that God wanted him to be a prophet. So one day he took a rucksack and packed up.

Kid pulls out a rucksack

    He was going to live in the desert – what do you think he packed?

(Take all suggestions. They usually think up suntan lotion, tent, provisions, etc.)

    What have you got in there, John?

John pulls out a Bible and a bottle of water

    Gosh! Well, good luck!

To the kids

    And he put the rucksack on his back and went off to pray to God in the desert.

See him off

    Goodbye, John!

John tramps off round the church

    There he goes.
    Do you think he's taken enough with him?
    (No!)
    Nor me. Well, let's see what happened.
    John got to the desert ...

John tramps back and looks round

    He knew this was the place where God wanted him to be, so he trusted that God would send him some food.
    And, sure enough, he found some wild honey.

He does so – ad lib:

    There you are, it says on the label – 'Wild Honey'.

Bounce off any kid who says it's obviously from the supermarket

    Look, give me a break.
    And then he found some nice yummy ...

John pounces on some grasshoppers

    grasshoppers (*Picture 2.1*).

John apparently eats one

    Then, as the nights are cold in the desert, John decided to make himself a camel skin coat. We're not too sure how he managed this.

8 Script 2 – St John the Baptist

Move over to flip-chart, and reveal a camel picture (Picture 2.2a)

  Perhaps a camel passed by one day and John …

Remove coat cut out from camel (Picture 2.2b)

  helped himself.

Ad lib a throwaway line

  Or perhaps somebody gave it to him. Then John reads his Bible …

John sits down quietly and reads his Bible.

  and said his prayers, and stayed alone in the desert, very close to God.
  And after a while he realized God wanted him to be His messenger to the people of Israel. So John packed up –

He does so

Ad lib   'Don't forget the grasshoppers!'
  And moved off to the River Jordan.

Exit John: watch him tramp off to the back of the church; if your font happens to be at the back, it would make a very suitable destination

  Now the point is – what was God's message?

Ask the deacon, or whoever reads the Gospel, to be ready with the answer, but let the kids have a go first. Establish that the message was 'Repent! For the kingdom of Heaven has come near!'

  'Repent! For the kingdom of Heaven has come near!'
  Hmm. What does 'repent' mean? I'll show you –
  Anyone here got a mobile?

Child with mobile comes forward and hands it to you

  Coo! Fantastic – I think I'll have that.

Pocket it. The child will say 'Hey!' or something, but don't make a meal of it, just turn to the others and say

  Should I have done that?
  (**No!**)
  No, you're right. It's very wrong to nick a mobile.
  I'm going to have to repent – that is, turn myself round …

Turn to face your victim

  That's what 'repent' means.
  And do my best to put things right. *(give the mobile back)*

To the child

        Sorry about that.

Look towards John

        So what was your message, John?
John   'Repent! For the kingdom of Heaven has come near!'
Preacher   I think that message is so important we ought to hear it again.

To congregation

        Let's all repent, turn ourselves round, and look at John – kids, can you show them how?

The children turn to face John, followed by the adults

        OK, John, let's hear the message again –
John   'Repent! For the kingdom of Heaven has come near!'
Preacher   How near?
John   Any minute now!
Preacher   OK, we'd better get on.

Ask everyone to turn back

        John lived 2,000 years ago – and he was right about the kingdom of Heaven – Jesus turned up almost at once.
        Come and join us, John –

John joins you down the front

        And John is still worth listening to, because the kingdom of Heaven that he preached *began* when Jesus came to live with us on Earth. Only Christians know that, but one day everybody will know about the kingdom of Heaven because it will appear, huge and wonderful, on the great day when Jesus comes again, at the end of time.
        When will that be, John?
John   Only God knows that![20]
Preacher   Right, we'll have to wait, the Kingdom could come at any time. The great thing is to repent and be ready. Just as John said.
        In the meantime, we don't have to wait until the end of time to meet Jesus again. He's here every time we break bread at the altar. Let's be ready to greet Him in Bread and Wine.

---

20 In performance, the child playing John said 'When Jesus comes back!', which was a very good (and accurate) answer.

Script 3   Christmas Crackers
(Christmas Day Script 1)

The following three sermons work with any of the Christmas Gospels, though – for a family service – it's better to keep to a narrative (like the visit of the shepherds in Luke 2) rather than John describing the Mystery of the Incarnation in John 1.

> **THEME**
>
> This is the perfect day for a Family Mass. The challenge is to give everyone – particularly the people who don't come to church very often – some nugget of the Christian faith to take away with them. Using a traditional prop, like Christmas crackers or a Christmas Tree, means you can end the sermon by saying, 'So when you get home and pull your crackers, or look at your tree, remember that …'

An extra devotion has been added, directed to the Infant Jesus.

SET UP
- Buy a box of crackers, checking first that they've got paper crowns inside.
- Gather the materials for an enormous home-made cracker for the children to pull at the end of the session, and put the cracker together. (Most party shops sell cracker kits, or you can get them online.) Place a plastic Bambino[21] inside or, if you're stuck, a card depicting the Infant Jesus.
- Put some Christmas cracker jokes in your pocket in case the ones in the crackers turn out to be unsuitable. Don't do too many, three max.

---

21 This is the traditional name for the little figure of Baby Jesus, placed in the Crib.

CRACKER JOKES FOR KIDS:

> Who hides in the bakery at Christmas?
> *A mince spy!*
> What do you get when you cross a snowman with a vampire?
> *Frostbite!*
> What do you sing at a snowman's birthday party?
> *Freeze a jolly good fellow!*
> What goes ho-ho whoosh, ho-ho whoosh?
> *Santa caught in a revolving door.*
> What kind of candle burns longer: a red candle or a green candle?
> *Neither, candles always burn shorter …*

ADDRESS

Gather the children, establish what day it is (CHRISTMAS!) and admire any toys that the kids bring up with them

> Well, I got a Christmas present as well –

Produce the box of crackers

> What are these?
> **(Christmas crackers!)**
> What do you do with them?
> **(Pull them)**
> OK, can anyone help me?

Pull cracker 1, and gather up the bits

> Fantastic, loved the bang! And it's got …

Hold the contents up

> a crown, and a joke and a present.
> Who wants to wear the crown?

If nobody volunteers, put it on one of the servers, or the vicar of course

> What about the present?

Hand the present to a kid who can be trusted not to swallow it

> What's the joke like?

Read it out

> Awful!

Script 3 – Christmas Crackers (Christmas Day Script 1)

Produce cracker 2

>Let's try another one …

Same business with crown and present, end with the joke

>They don't get any better, do they?
>Do you know why we pull crackers at Christmas?

Produce cracker 3 – this is the home-made cracker

>First, because Christmas starts with a BANG. The first Christmas had loads of angels in the sky, singing at the top of their voices.

Pull it

>And secondly because they've got jokes inside.

Read out another joke – react to the groan

>Come on, guys, laugh! It's Christmas.
>And – this is really important – we pull because they contain a present.

Produce the Bambino, ask a child to hold it up

>That reminds us that God sent us an amazing present at Christmas –
>His only Son, Jesus Christ
>And, lastly, because they've got a crown –

Put it on the Bambino

>That reminds us that Baby Jesus is the King of the World.
>So, when you pull a cracker today.
>remember that.
>Christmas is about God appearing with a BANG!
>That God sent us a present – Baby Jesus!
>that He's the King of the World,
>AND that we're so happy, we even laugh at Christmas cracker jokes –
>Let's try one more …

Do so

>Happy Christmas!

CHRISTMAS EXTRA

In a small congregation you can gather the kids – and adults – in a circle down the front and add a devotion to the Infant Jesus.[22] Alert the musicians (if you've got some) to what you are going to do and ask for some mood music

Take the Bambino from the Crib, hold it very gently, and say something on the lines of:

Preacher Look how small Baby Jesus is.
That's how small God became.
So small that He had to be looked after,
and held carefully.

Hold the Bambino as you would a real baby – and kiss it

Can you look after Baby Jesus?

Hand the Bambino to a responsive kid

That's super, let's pass Him round.
As you hold the baby, remember that God became this little for you.
You can pray to Jesus, or thank Him, or just give this image of Him a kiss.
Anything you like …

Pass the Bambino round the group as somebody plays some quiet music.

---

22 This devotion, of passing the Bambino round a group, is very common in Southern Italy.

Script 4 Christmas Tree

(Christmas Day Script 2)

> **THEME**
>
> Like the Christmas cracker homily that precedes this, the address below focuses on another familiar Christmas prop, the Christmas Tree. This means you can get to the classic line which ends most Christmas homilies, 'so when you get home, look at your Tree, and remember that …'

An extra devotion has been added, directed to the Infant Jesus.

THE CHRISTMAS TREE

SET UP

- Buy a small Christmas Tree, put it in a pot, and pat some earth round it.
- Place the decorations (listed below) into a small cardboard box, and have two adults ready to give the kids a hand as they decorate the tree.

You will need:

- An angel for the top (not a fairy …).
- Gold and silver balls, plus one green or one blue one.
- Any Christmas decorations that represent human beings and animals – little nut-cracker soldiers, kings, queens, gingerbread men, donkeys, rocking horses, cockerels. They can be cute wooden toys or foil-covered chocolates. But don't include Father Christmas, he just confuses the issue.
- Food or fruits of the Earth – sweeties, gingerbread (not gingerbread men, they go in the category above), decorative cherries or apples (artificial ones are fine), anything that can notionally be eaten.
- Little gilt trumpets, toy drums, any sort of musical instrument, little angels.
- Wrapped presents for the base of the Tree.
- A Bambino (the image of the Christ Child from the crib) concealed in an attractive scarf.

ADDRESS

Bring the tree and the box of decorations to the front

TREES

> I've brought a tree into church this morning. Does anyone know what it is?
> **(A Christmas Tree)**
> Yup, a Christmas Tree.
> This sort of tree is also called an 'evergreen' – can you guess why?

Take them through the fresh green pine needles, their nice smell, etc.

> An evergreen looks green in winter just as it does during the rest of the year.
> It's a super thing to have in winter, it reminds us that one day spring will come back and all the trees will look green again.
> Have you got one in your house?
> **(Yes!)**
> Does it look like this?

Depends on how literal the kids are; establish that their trees are decorated

> OK, let's decorate this one.

Pull forward the box of decorations

DECORATING THE TREE

> Right, now this tree isn't any old tree, it's a *Christmas* tree and has to be decorated properly.
> You see, a Christmas Tree is rather like the world God made.
> It's fresh and alive and looks good.
> So let's think of God's world.
> Let's start with the universe. I need something on this Tree that's going to remind me of the planets – what have we got?

Get some kids to find and put up the gold and silver balls

> OK, and we need one planet to be Earth.
> Does anyone know what colour the Earth looks like from space?
> **(Blue or green)**
> Have we got a blue ball? Good show, let's put that up …
> And the Earth is full of living things, animals for example – have we got any animals?

Put them up – reserve the human beings

And of course there are all the things that God gave us to eat –

Put up the sweets, fruits, etc.

And most important there are human beings. Have we got any of those?
(**Yes!**)

Hang up the little toys; have a couple of them close enough together to bash into each other when they are swung

God loved the human beings He'd made and He gave them lots of presents. Let's put them round –

Stack the wrapped presents round the base

PRESENTS

What sort of presents does God give us? *(this is rhetorical)*

Mums and Dads
People to love us
Stuff to play with
Legs to run round on. *(keep it snappy …)*
OK, so we must imagine God looking at the universe
and thinking He'd done a good job, all those planets,
and the animals and …
the people – oh, no, wait a moment – some of the people aren't behaving too well –

Swing one of the human decorations so it bangs into another – look up at the kids

I think he did that on purpose.
Goodness, there goes another one –

(Bang)

'Hmm,' said God. 'The humans are behaving badly.
They're going to make themselves very unhappy.
I think I'd better send them another present'
So God sent an Angel …
Have we got an angel? Great, let's put the angel in Heaven.

Put the angel on the top of the tree

And God filled the sky with music and angels singing.

Put on angels, drums and any other instruments

> And the angels told some shepherds that God had sent them a brilliant Christmas present – here it is –

Place the wrapped Bambino among the presents

> What do you think it is?

Ask a child to unwrap it gently

> Who is it?
> **(Baby Jesus)**

Pick up the Bambino

> Baby Jesus, God's own Son – who came down from Heaven itself

Hold up the Bambino and bring it down

> Right down to the Earth, to be with us.

Place the Bambino back among the presents

> Look where I've put Baby Jesus – at the bottom of the Tree, right here where its roots go into the Earth. That's a long way down.

WRAPPING IT UP

> So when you go home, look at your Tree and I bet you'll find you've got some of this story on it. Silver balls, things to eat, perhaps you've even got an Angel at the top?

(**Optional** *if one of the children says they've got a star at the top.*)

> A star is fine – that's another way that God told us about Baby Jesus.
> He sent a Star to shine over the stable where Jesus was born.
> Then there're the presents at the bottom. They're really important. They remind us of the presents God gives us at Christmas: a beautiful Christmas Tree, lights, stars, sweets and best of all, His Son Jesus Christ.
> Merry Christmas!

Script 4 – Christmas Tree (Christmas Day Script 2)

CHRISTMAS EXTRA

See page 13.

Script 5 Speaking Animals
(Christmas Day Script 3)

> **THEME**
>
> This sermon takes off from the legend that domestic animals can talk on Christmas Eve. (It's considered very unlucky to hear them: they are scathing about their human owners and very good at guessing who's going to die in the year ahead.) This session requires an agreeable floppy toy sheep, the sort that you can manipulate to shake its head, and talk in your ear, and generally upstage you. You will need to supplement the normal animals in your crib set (the ox and ass) with a shepherd's dog (toy huskies are fine) and any feasible stuffed animal you can lay your hands on. Plastic birds work – but not plastic dinosaurs (tempting though they are …). This is because, after the comic turn with the sheep, people are quite moved as they hear what the animals brought to the Manger.

SET UP

- The ox and ass from your Crib set plus extra animals placed with them in the Crib.
- A large floppy toy sheep.

BEFORE THE SERVICE

Ask a couple of adults to be on hand if you need to bring any of the Crib figures forward.

GOSPEL Luke 2.1–16

Make whatever cuts are necessary, but bring the Shepherds to the Manger.

Script 5 – Speaking Animals (Christmas Day Script 3)

ADDRESS

Ad lib Merry Christmas and admire any toys that the children may show you

> Well, I got a present too – this lamb.

Produce the toy sheep

> I'm going to call him Worthy …

Wait to see if any grown-up gets this dreadful joke and give them a look

> Yup, Worthy is the lamb …
> I'll put him down here *(Worthy appears to protest)*
> – nope, Worthy, stay!

Plonk him down

> Right. Now I'd like to talk about animals this morning because, I expect you know, they behave very strangely at Christmas. I was told by a little Australian girl that in Australia Father Christmas's sleigh is pulled by kangaroos … Can you imagine it?
> I looked at her in amazement and I said,
> 'But kangaroos can't fly!'
> 'Neither can reindeer …!' she replied.

Pause for a second, oh yeah, nor they can …

> Of course she was right, it had never crossed my mind. Well, we need to think about reindeer – and kangaroos – because animals are important at Christmas.

> That's because when God entered our world as a human being, He came to the world He loved. He loved every living being in it. Us of course – but also reindeer and kangaroos, and cats, and donkeys and sheep – everything.
> It's why we have an ox and an ass in every crib scene.
> Here they are …

Bring the ox and the ass forward

> And I'll tell you something else, the animals know God loves them. In fact, one of the stories we tell at Christmas is that – on Christmas Eve – the animals can talk. Every one of them, the ox and the ass – and that sheepdog with the shepherd – can you see him?

Bring the toy dog forward

> And the goat. *(or whatever you've got with the other shepherd)*

Bring it forward

Even this lamb …

Pick up Worthy, who waves a front leg at the kids

They can all talk. In fact, this one has been talking non-stop since midnight …

Glare at the sheep

But the point is – and you need to understand this – only priests[23] can hear what they say …

(Anticipate groan from congregation)

The sheep lunges at your ear

Just a minute …

Listen

OK, yes, Worthy says hello, boys and girls.

Worthy talks to you again, you answer him

Oh, I'm sure they like you.
Do you like Worthy, kids?
(**Yes!**) *(but don't wait for a reply)*
OK, well, Worthy, it's Christmas Day, the day when God came down to Earth as a little child.

You and Worthy turn to look at the Bambino

Did you give anything to Baby Jesus?

Worthy talks in your ear

Oh, you gave your wool to make Him a blanket – that was really nice of you!

From now on, somebody holds up the animals as you ask Worthy what each one gave Baby Jesus. Adapt this to what you've got

The donkey carried Mary to Bethlehem.
The ox gave Jesus his Manger to sleep in.
The sheepdog guided the shepherd to the Manger.
The goat *(cow/extra sheep)* gave Jesus some of her milk.

---

23 Or deacons, or readers, or whatever title you can lay hold of. It might just be 'grown-ups'.

Script 5 – Speaking Animals (Christmas Day Script 3)

>Some birds gave their feathers for His pillow.
>Some bees formed a line and hummed a Christmas carol.
>The doves cooed Jesus to sleep.
>A cat slept on Mary's feet and kept her warm.
>And the lion *(supposing you can find a toy one)* – the king of the beasts – arrived to greet the newborn King, and give Him a kiss …

When you've finished, Worthy looks as though he wants to talk again

>What is it, Worthy?

Listen

>Oh. *(to the kids)* Worthy would like to ask us a question.

Listen

>Worthy wants to know what *we've* given Jesus this Christmas.
>That's a good question!
>Well, we've given Jesus something that every human baby needs – something it wouldn't survive a day without – we've given Jesus our love.
>That's why we're all here this morning.

Give Worthy to a child to hold and hold up the image of Jesus, the Bambino from the Crib

>And Jesus has given us something too. Let's look at Him.
>Jesus was born today to show us that God loves us.
>Just at the moment He's a little baby, so we hold him carefully.

Cradle the baby

>But when He grows up He's going to show us how much *He* loves us, and how tough love can be. But right now He's only little.
>So I'm going to hold this little image of Jesus carefully, and I'm going to say a prayer to the Christ Child.

Pray over the Bambino and, as you say 'Amen', kiss it

Depending on numbers, see if the children would like to pass the Bambino round, very carefully, and make their own silent prayer to Jesus

Offer a couple of suggestions

>You could say 'Happy Birthday, Jesus', or tell Him your name, or how old you are … very quietly.

End by putting the figures (including Worthy) back in the Crib, the Bambino last; kneel and either say a very short prayer to the Christ child – or ask the children to join you in singing 'Away in a Manger'.

Script 6   The Naming of Jesus
(The Naming and Circumcision of Jesus)

Luke 2.15–21

> **NAMES**
>
> Today marks the circumcision and naming of the Infant Jesus.
> The meaning of 'Jesus', and the command by Gabriel that He should be so named, is put on hold in this session. Instead we focus on names themselves, scary and otherwise – why you don't call your teacher 'Steve', why the Jews didn't call God by His Name, and how lucky we are that God chose to have an ordinary human name when He came to live among us: Jesus/Joshua/Josh.

SET UP

- A1 flip-chart and Pictures 6.1–6.5 from www.canterburypress.co.uk/downloads.
- Black and red marker pens.

ADDRESS

Start by asking a kid her name[24]

> No, don't tell me, let me guess – you're Ermintrude …
> (**No!**)
> Aren't you? OK, I'll try again.
> You're Blodwyn?
> (**No!**)
> OK, I give up, what is your name?
> Polly! Of course, good to see you, Polly.

To the children

> You see, I can't guess somebody's name by just looking at them.

---

24 The names above are currently unfashionable, these things change overnight … choose some that are deeply uncool.

Script 6 – The Naming of Jesus (The Naming and Circumcision of Jesus)

> That's quite useful, because sometimes it can be dangerous to let somebody know who you are …

You might be able to ad lib some devastating story. (Mine is my first encounter with the sports teacher. I'd spent the term getting into trouble one way or another, but I thought she wouldn't know about that. However, when she heard my name, she gave me a look and said, 'Oh, so you're Sarah Lenton!')

> And if you're talking to somebody important, you think twice before you call them by their Christian name –
> Supposing you met the Queen, for example, what would you call her? (**Your Majesty, Ma'am**)
> And what do you call your teacher? (**Mrs/Mr/Miss So and So**)
> And what do we call God?
> Has He got a name?

If there's a stricken silence, move on to the story; if they say 'Jesus', add

> Yes, God was given a Name when He came to Earth – we're going to think about that – but what about before He came here? I'm going to tell you a story …

MOSES AND THE BURNING BUSH

Flip-chart – stick up the pictures of Moses and his sheep (Pictures 6.1 & 6.2)

> One day a very long time ago, a shepherd was looking after his sheep when he saw something odd.

(Picture 6.3)

> A bush, which had flames shooting out of it

Draw some red flames

> but was not burnt up.
> 'That's weird,' said the shepherd, and he went to see what was happening. Then something *really* weird happened – the bush spoke –

Write up 'MOSES!'

> 'Moses!' said the bush.

The sheep make a rapid exit

> 'That's me,' said the shepherd.
> 'Come closer, take off your shoes – this is holy ground …'
> So Moses knelt by the bush and a Voice from inside the bush said, 'I am the God of Abraham and Isaac – '

Script 6 – The Naming of Jesus (The Naming and Circumcision of Jesus)

('I know those names,' thought Moses, 'they're the names of my ancestors!')
' – and I've chosen you to lead my people away from this country, to another that I will show you.'
'Oh!' said Moses, and he thought for a moment.
'The trouble is,' he said. 'I don't think anyone would listen to me. Who, should I say, *told* me to lead them? Lord God, have you got a Name?'
'I Am who I Am,' said the Voice.
'If anyone asks you who told you to lead my people,
tell them that I Am *(write it up)* sent you.'

Look at the picture

So there you are, we've got two names – 'Moses' and 'I Am'.

YAHWEH

Of course, God didn't speak to Moses in English, He spoke to him in Moses' own language, which was Hebrew.
God's Name in Hebrew looks like this –

Write in the Hebrew

יהוה

H W H Y

Ad lib that's it in Hebrew and Hebrew is written right to left. Put the letters in the 'right' order: **YHWH**

God's Name is pronounced 'Yahweh'

Write 'Yahweh'

Vowels

If anyone notices the lack of vowels, explain ancient Hebrew only has consonants; that's usually perfectly OK – write up your name just using consonants. If your name is actually unrecognizable with only consonants, then you've got the perfect opportunity to say, 'But it can be awkward sometimes. It's what makes reading the Bible so interesting.'

The Jews are very glad that they know the Name of God,
but they never say it,
and they never write it out in full. It's too holy.

> *Our Father*
>
> **Christians also hesitate to use the Name of God, they just refer to it: 'Our Father, who art in Heaven, hallowed be thy Name …**

Well, when God came to Earth at Christmas, everything changed.

Put up picture (Picture 6.4) of the Infant Jesus

He was so little He needed grown-ups to look after Him.

Add Mary and Joseph (Picture 6.5)

Do you know their names?
(**Mary and Joseph**)
Yup, and one of the first things Mary and Joseph did was give the Baby a name. What was it?
(**Jesus**)

Write it up

Jesus, just an ordinary human name – it's the same name as Joshua – anyone here called Josh? Well, you've got Jesus' name.
And when Jesus grew up, He said,
'If anyone prays to God the Father in my Name,
He will grant their request.'
Which is why we so often end our prayers by saying,
'We pray this in the Name of your Son, Jesus Christ.'
It's good to know that we can pray to God using the same name Mary used when she called the kid Jesus in to supper.
Let's do that now:

Jesus, Son of God
Pray for us
Jesus, Son of Mary
Pray for us
Jesus, friend of sinners
Pray for us
Jesus, friend of children
Pray for us

Let us pray.
Almighty God, may we – who love the Holy Name of Jesus – enjoy His friendship in this life and come at last to your Kingdom, where He lives and reigns with you and the Holy Spirit, for ever and ever. **Amen**

Script 7 The Holy Family

This address can be used for the Feast of the Holy Family, Holy Baptism, or any Gospel of the day that mentions Jesus' family.

THEME

The theme is Jesus' family – His actual one, plus the one He has gathered to Himself. The session gives us a sidebar on the status of Jesus' 'brothers and sisters'. The Greek words for 'brother' and 'sister' can refer to a sibling or to relations in an extended family – cousins, step-brothers, foster sisters, and so on. The doctrine of the Perpetual Virginity of Our Lady[25] suggests that Jesus' siblings were actually step-relations and, given the complexity of modern family life, it might be helpful to suggest that Our Lord's family wasn't necessarily a solid nuclear unit. The session can also be useful if you want to launch a Food Bank or some such charitable drive.

SET UP

- A1 flip-chart, marker pen.
- Pictures 7.1–7.8 from www.canterburypress.co.uk/downloads.

ADDRESS

Ad lib on whatever Sunday it is: the jumping off point is

> Jesus grew up in an ordinary family. I mean *really* ordinary – He had a mum and a dad and the house was full of kids. Let's run through Jesus' family …

---

[25] This doctrine has been orthodox for centuries, assumed by the Fathers of the Church from the fourth century, and not disturbed by the Reformers in the sixteenth century.

HOME LIFE IN NAZARETH

Put up Picture 7.1

Does anyone know what Jesus' Mum was called?
(Mary) *(Picture 7.2)*
And His Dad?
(Joseph) *(Picture 7.3)*
There were loads of other children in the house as well, because in those days people lived with their cousins and step-brothers and sisters, and they were all lumped together. Jesus grew up with four other boys, called: James, Joseph, Simon and Judas,[26] *(Picture 7.4)*, and there were so many girls nobody ever seems to have counted them. *(Picture 7.5)*

> ### For Older Children
>
> **Jesus' actual Father was God. Joseph was His step-father. The Greek word for brother/sister can be used to describe any bunch of kids growing up together, including extended family, step-brothers and sisters, and cousins.**

Jesus also had aunties and uncles, *(Picture 7.6)* and He grew up just like you and me.
Who do you suppose told Him to eat His nice chicken soup?
(His Mum/Mary)
Or tidy His bedroom?
(His Mum/Mary)
And who took Him to the Synagogue?
(Mary and Joseph)
We don't know if Jesus ever quarrelled with His brothers and sisters, but He seemed to all the neighbours to be just another kid.

> ### Jesus, the Boy Next Door
>
> We know Jesus was an ordinary boy because, when He grew up, and went round teaching people about God, His neighbours said, 'Hey, where did He get all this from? Isn't this *Jesus*? The carpenter's son?' *(Matthew 13.53–57)*

---

[26] Matthew 13.55.

FAMILIES

> Let's talk about families. Have you noticed how they tend to look like each other?

Ad lib an anecdote about some likeness in your own family; it needn't be facial, it could be a trait: 'I knew he was your brother as soon as he annoyed me …'

Look round at the families present – ask some siblings to stand up

> Do people think you look alike?
> What do you think?

Back to all the kids

> You are like your family because you are with them a lot.
> Like this one – they're called the Skinflints. (*Picture 7.7*)
> The Skinflints were very fond of each other and stayed together.
> They locked the front door,
> and stacked up the fridge,
> and they made jolly sure nobody got any of their stuff.
> They looked after themselves – and ended up looking like this.

Draw in Skinflint faces (on template)

> They look very suspicious, don't they?
> Even the cat …

Draw in the cat's expression

> If anyone said to them, 'Hey, why don't you lighten up?'
> they'd say, 'Ah, it's not the Skinflint way …'
> But Jesus thought that however much you love your family, you don't have to stop there.
> There are lots of other people who can be part of your family and you can end up being like each other, not because you have the same name – or the same nose – but because you do the same things.

GOSPEL

If the Gospel of the day happens to be Matthew 12.46, Mark 4.1–9 or Luke 8.4–8, you could split the homily here, read the Gospel, and go on to Part 2 below. Otherwise paraphrase it:

> Once, when Jesus was preaching, His family turned up and asked Him to stop embarrassing them and come home.
> People round Him said, 'Hey, Jesus, your family's here!' And Jesus replied, 'Really? Who are my family? I tell you anyone who hears the Word of God and does it, they're my family – my mother and sister and brother.'

ADDRESS Part 2

> So here's a picture of Jesus' family. (*Picture 7.8*)
> All these people have listened to the Word of God, and obeyed it. They've thrown open their doors, and shared their stuff and, though they're very different from each other *(point that out)* and some speak Russian, or French or English, they're all family and they look like it.

Turn to somebody in the clergy or serving team – that is, somebody you can trust ...

	What do you think they look like?
Server	I think they look happy.
Preacher	Yup, I agree, can you draw that?

Server draws a smile on one of the faces. Ask the kids to fill in the others – don't forget the cat

> So it's up to us. Of course, we'll always have our own families, but we can join Jesus' family anytime. To do that, we listen to what He says – and have a go at doing it.

From here you can springboard into:

HOLY BAPTISM

> And now we are going to welcome *Name* into the Christian family by taking them to the font and baptizing them.

CHARITY PROJECT

> And now *Name* is going to tell us how we can help poorer families.

ON WITH THE MASS

> So, as Jesus' family, let's get ready to meet Him at the Family Meal round the altar.

Script 8 The Three Gifts
(Epiphany Script 1)
Matthew 2.1–12

THEME

The Wise Men – as mysterious as their presents: we don't even know how many Magi there were, but their gifts suggest three. This session looks again at those famous gifts and what they tell us about the Christ Child. If ever there was a time to use incense at a Family Mass, this is it.

SET UP

- A1 flip-chart.
- One large present wrapped up – something deeply unsuitable as a normal present, like a plastic cudgel or battle axe or plastic scythe, anything you might have used at halloween – it is not labelled.
- The Bambino from your crib set and either the three Kings, or three kids to represent them.
- If you are using children for this, have three crowns ready (paper ones from a Christmas cracker are fine), and try to rehearse with them quickly beforehand.
- The three gifts: gold bling in a box, or a box covered in gold paper; a jar of sweet-smelling oil/ointment (or myrrh oil which you can get online or at a cathedral gift shop); incense grains in an incense boat.
- A thurible already primed with lit charcoal.
- Pictures 8.1–8.6 www.canterburypress.co.uk/downloads.
- Brightly coloured marker pens.

GOSPEL   Matthew 2.1–12

Read the Gospel as you would at any Eucharist and honour it with the Kings' third gift of incense. If your church does not use incense, beg or borrow a thurible – plus some incense and charcoal – from one that does. (Your congregation will probably register it as an exotic extra to the Feast Day.)

Script 8 – The Three Gifts (Epiphany Script 1)

ADDRESS

Come forward with the unlabelled present. Ad lib about Christmas: the tree and the presents

> Did any of you get presents?

React to the show of hands and let a couple of kids tell you what they got. Bring forward the unlabelled present

> I've opened all my presents except this one.
> It hasn't got a label …
> I don't really know who it's for *(turn it)* –
> Shall we open it anyway?

Ask a child to unwrap it, and stagger back at what's inside

> Goodness! Who could this be for?
> It must be *Name* …

Anyone unsuitable – the vicar is the obvious target; hand it over

> It's really important to label presents.
> There are some people I know who got all their presents muddled up.

Reveal Pictures 8.1–8.6 on the flip-chart: Jimmy, Nan and Tibby are at the bottom, their presents (with a square of wrapping paper placed over each one) are at the top. Run through the recipients: Jimmy is a kid, Nan is his granny, and Tibby a very uncompromising cat

> So when Nan opened her present on Christmas Day she got – ?

Ask a kid to unwrap Nan's present

> – An inter-galactic space blaster! *(or whatever you want to call the power water pistol revealed)* Picture 8.4.
> And Jimmy got – ?

Same business

> – A cat basket! *Picture 8.5.*
> And Tibby got – ? *Picture 8.6.*

Same business

> – A nice pink woolly jumper!
> Who should have got the water pistol? Can you show me?

Ask a kid to draw a line from Jimmy to the pistol

> And who should have got the jumper?

Same business, this time the line goes to Nan

> And – this is the difficult one – who should have got the cat basket?

Same business, line drawn to Tibby

> That's better: when you give presents you want to make sure they're just right for the person you are giving them to.

THREE KINGS

> Well, this Sunday is called Epiphany Sunday,[27] and it's the day the three Kings came to Bethlehem and gave gifts to Baby Jesus. Let's meet them.

Bring the three Kings forward and give them their names. (If you are using crib figures: Caspar is young, Balthazar is a Moor, and Melchior is old.)

> Well, the three Kings naturally wanted to give Jesus the right presents, and they talked about it before they set out.

Narrate this bit – put a hand on the shoulder of each king as you talk about him or her

> 'Jesus is a King,' said Caspar. 'I want to give Him a present fit for a King.'
>
> 'Jesus is a human being,' said Balthazar. 'I want to give Him a present for a Man.'
>
> 'Jesus is God,' said Melchior. 'What on earth am I going to give God?'

THE KINGS' PRESENTS

> Here are the three presents –

Bring them forward

> Which one do you think Caspar gave Jesus – the 'present fit for a King'?

*You might have to steer them – it's **gold***

---

27 Epiphany means 'manifestation' or 'showing', a moment when it becomes apparent who Jesus is. There are traditionally three epiphanies, celebrated one after the other in the Christmas season: the epiphany to the Gentiles – represented by the Kings; the Baptism of Our Lord, when the Father acclaimed Jesus as His Beloved Son; and Jesus' first miracle at Cana, when He revealed Himself to be God.

34 Script 8 – The Three Gifts (Epiphany Script 1)

Give Caspar the gold, or place it by the Caspar figure.

> And what about the other two? Let's look at them.
> This is **myrrh** – it's an oil and smells lovely …

Smear a little on a child's palm

> This is used to anoint the dead.
> And this is **frankincense**.

Open the boat

> It looks like little bits of glue.

Take out a pinch and let the children see it

> But when you throw it on to hot charcoal it becomes a beautifully scented smoke.
> We use frankincense when we want to show that things are holy.
> So, we've got the right present for God.
> What's the right present for a human being?
> **(Myrrh)**
> One day Jesus would die, and the myrrh could be used to anoint Him.

Give Balthazar the myrrh

> And that leaves …?
> **(Frankincense)**
> The present for God.

Give Melchior the frankincense

GIFTS FOR THE CHRIST CHILD

> So when the three Kings found Baby Jesus,
> they knelt in front of Him.

Bring the Bambino forward, ask the Kings to kneel. (Or arrange the crib figures round the Christ Child.)

> Caspar gave Him gold. *(he does)*
> And Balthazar gave Him myrrh. *(he does)*
> And Melchior gave Him frankincense. *(he does)*
> I think we'll use a bit of Melchior's frankincense to bless our image of Baby Jesus we've got here, and watch the smoke go up towards Heaven as we pray.

Fill up the thurible, ask all the children to kneel, and cense the Bambino as you pray

> Lord God,
> Today three kings knelt before your Son and offered Him their gifts.
> We would like to give Jesus some gifts as well.
> Our love,
> our thanks,
> and our hearts.
> Accept our prayer through Jesus our Lord,
> Who lives with you and the Holy Spirit. **Amen**

POSTSCRIPT

'Bethlehem of Noblest Cities' will work well as the Offertory or Recessional after this homily – particularly verse 4 – 'solemn things of mystic meaning …'.

Script 9   Useful Presents
(Epiphany Script 2)

> **USEFUL PRESENTS**
>
> In some ways, the Kings' gifts can appear deeply unsuitable – who would give a toddler myrrh? And yet they can just as easily be seen as representing the necessities of life.

SET UP

- Three cardboard boxes (wine boxes from the supermarket are perfect).
- Cover them with Christmas wrapping paper and label them 'Gold', 'Frankincense' and 'Myrrh'.
- Keep the top of each box open and fill it with:
- Gold – some gold coins (you can get cheap pirate coins from party suppliers), packets of food, a jumper, socks, soap, and a bar of chocolate.
- Frankincense – beautiful things: an incense boat, jewellery (bling will do), music (any musical instrument or a CD), a picture (a postcard from an Art Gallery), an icon (preferably of the Blessed Virgin Mary and Jesus), and a bar of chocolate.
- Myrrh – medicine, ointment, packet of plasters, bandages and a bar of chocolate.
- Set the three boxes at the back of the church and depute three kids to bring them up on cue. If you've got crowns, or any dressing-up gear for the Kings, they'll look very impressive – but don't worry if you haven't.
- The children should bring the boxes up with the names on the boxes hidden (they clutch that side to their tummy), so they can turn and reveal the labels on cue.
- Somebody to help you field the presents as you unpack the boxes.
- A1 flip-chart and marker pen.
- Blackboard chalk in a small open container, one piece for each child. (Chalk can be bought in stationery and art shops.)
- Epiphany chalk cards, Picture 9.1, printed up from www.canterburypress.co.uk/downloads.

Script 9 – Useful Presents (Epiphany Script 2)   37

GOSPEL   Matthew 2.1–12

ADDRESS

Ad lib on the feast day

> Today we are celebrating the Epiphany.[28]
> Does anyone know what that means?
> What happened on the first Epiphany?
> **(The three Kings/Wise Men came to see Baby Jesus)**
> Yes, some Kings turned up.
> They came later than the Shepherds.
> In fact, when you read about them in the Gospel, it looks as if Mary, Joseph and the baby had moved out of the stable and into somebody's house. Jesus was probably a toddler by the time they arrived.
> People have always loved the three Kings, they are grave and mysterious and give Jesus strange presents.
> Does anyone know their names?

Children often know this – especially if they have been singing 'We Three Kings of Orient Are' recently. However you get the information, write the names up on the flip-chart, in this order, and with a large capital letter at the start of each name

> <u>C</u>aspar
> <u>B</u>althazar
> <u>M</u>elchior

> Goodness, their names are as strange as their presents.
> I think we should meet them.

Cue the children up from the back; some 'play-in' music from the organist would go well, but don't let it drag. Range the children down the front; they should be in Gold, Myrrh and Frankincense order. It doesn't matter if they're not, but open the boxes in that order

> Well, the first King was Caspar and he[29] gave baby Jesus –

The first child holds up his/her box

---

28 Epiphany means 'manifestation' or 'showing', a moment when it becomes apparent who Jesus is. There are traditionally three epiphanies, celebrated one after the other in the Christmas season: the epiphany to the Gentiles – represented by the Kings; the Baptism of Our Lord, when the Father acclaimed Jesus as His Beloved Son; and Jesus' first miracle at Cana, when He revealed Himself to be God.

29 It's less muddling to call the Kings 'he' even if they are played by girls. Cross-dressing is a venerable Christmas tradition.

Gold.
That was a really useful present.

Hold up the coins

Mary and Joseph and Baby Jesus were just about to escape to Egypt. They were going to be refugees and they needed gold – money – for all the necessities of life; things like –

Pull out these things as you mention them

Food, and warm clothes, and socks, and soap and, of course – chocolate!
The second King was Balthazar, and he gave Baby Jesus –

The kid holds up his box

Myrrh.
That was another useful present.

Hold up the ointment

Myrrh is a spice made into an ointment, it's used to anoint sick people. Mary and Joseph were going to need –

Pull out these things

Medicine, and pills, and plasters, and bandages, and – of course – chocolate!
There's nothing better for an invalid than chocolate.
The third King was Melchior. He gave Baby Jesus –

The kid holds up his box

Frankincense.
And that's a useful present too. Frankincense *(hold up the incense boat)* is incense. It has a beautiful holy smell, and we need beautiful things in our lives, just as much as we need food and medicine. Things like –

Pull them out

Jewellery, and music, and pictures, and icons and – of course – *(the kids will be anticipating this)* that most beautiful of presents, chocolate!
So the Holy Family were given food, and medicine, and beauty, by their three visitors. Wonderful gifts. I think we'd like some of these presents ourselves.

Cue in applause for the kids and allow them to exit. You will probably find that all eyes are on the chocolate – offer to distribute it after Mass

EPIPHANY CHALK

Ever since that first Epiphany, people have wanted the three Kings to turn up at their houses as well.
In Spain, little children are given presents from the three Kings.
But the rest of us are just happy to chalk up their names on our doors.

Over to the flip-chart

We do it by putting the initials of the Kings in a row:
C B M.
And placing the year at the begining and end
20 C B M 22.
And filling in the gaps with crosses
20 + C + B + M + 22.
C B M means Caspar, Melchior and Balthazar.
But it also means something else:

Write up 'Christus Mansionem Benedicat' with the initial letters in capitals

Christus Mansionem Benedicat, which means 'May Christ bless this dwelling'.
At the end of Mass, we'll bless some Epiphany Chalk, so you can chalk up the names of the Kings on the place where you live and ask for God's blessing on your home.

(The inscription can be chalked up over the front door, the main door, a nearby wall – anywhere actually)

BLESSING THE EPIPHANY CHALK

Priest	Our help is in the Name of the Lord.
All	**Who made Heaven and Earth.**
Priest	The Lord be with you.
All	**And with your spirit.**
Priest	Bless ✠ O Lord God, this chalk. And grant that they who use it to write the names of Caspar, Melchior and Balthazar on their homes may, through the prayers of your saints, enjoy health of body and protection of soul. Through Christ our Lord.
All	**Amen.**

The chalk is sprinkled with Holy Water. Dish out the chalk and the Epiphany Chalk Cards at the end of Mass

Script 10 The Baptism of Our Lord in a Family Eucharist that includes Holy Baptism

(A) Matthew 3.1, 6, 13–17
(B) Mark 1.9–11
(C) Luke 3.3, 7a, 21–22

THEME

This sermon uses a traditional tie-up between Jesus' Baptism and the story of Noah's Ark.[30] In this version of the Gospel, the Ark and the Church represent safe havens for human beings, entered at the expense of getting very wet. The session works best with a reasonable number of children present (to be the animals in the Ark).

SET UP

- A couple of people to help you stage manage the children, and sway on cue.
- Enough adults in the congregation who can be trusted to click their fingers and stamp their feet on cue to simulate rain.
- A box or chest with a lid.
- A short length of carpet to act as a gangplank.

Optional

- Somebody to play God – only cast this if you can be sure the actor is up to it. God should sound very clear and measured. Otherwise, incorporate God's speech into your story-telling.

---

30 These stories are linked by the tie-up between water and death, something that God's people – and, supremely, God's Son – overcome.

BEFORE THE ADDRESS

> There's going to be a lot of weather in this homily, I'm going to need some help.

Run a rehearsal with the adults and children. Clicking fingers for rain, stamping their feet for more rain, and various animal noises (see below). Establish that your hand coming down cues them in, and a finger across the throat 'kills' the sound.

ADDRESS

> Today we heard how Jesus was baptized in the River Jordan. Has anyone here seen somebody being baptized?

(Take what comes and run swiftly through what happens, establish that the priest pours water over the baby)

> Does the baby like it?

Run with that, and end by saying

> Well, whatever the baby thinks, God's love for us can mean us getting very wet indeed. We're going to hear another story today in which people get drenched.
> OK, this all happened a long time ago when people didn't seem to know or care very much about God – except one chap. His name was Noah.
> Anyone here want to be Noah?

Welcome Noah and stand him/her beside you

> OK, this is Noah. *(look at the kid appraisingly and then turn to the congregation)*
> You can see how good he is.
> Well, Noah had a family – anyone want to join Noah's family?

Choose Mrs Noah, Ham, Seth and Japheth. If you are going to run out of kids, just pick two – Mrs Noah and Ham (kids are usually amused by being called Ham). Line them up

> And they were very good too, just like Noah.
> Then one day it began to rain …

Cue in finger clicking for rain drops, then kill it

> And God spoke to Noah.

God   Noah, I'm going to make it rain. It's going to flood the Earth, and I want you to build an enormous boat to save yourself.

Preacher   So Noah and his family started to build a boat.

Noah and co. 'hammer' a clenched fist on the palm of the other hand

God   Bigger than that!

The kids spread out a bit (still in line) and keep hammering

>Much bigger –

Noah moves to one end of the sanctuary step, while Mrs Noah and Ham go to the other end

>Excellent! The boat is just right, you can stop.
>Now, I want you to get two of every animal there is into the boat –

Roll down the gangplank and look at the kids

Preacher   Anyone want to be an animal?
>How about a sheep?
>Anyone know what noise a sheep makes?
>(Baa)
>Brilliant, I need two sheep – can you join Noah in the boat?

The kids run up the gangplank and form a line along the sanctuary step. Add more animals. The rule is the kids can only be an animal if they can make a feasible noise, or look like the animal in some way. (Giraffes will test their ingenuity.) They come in pairs – you may need to rope in some parents – and line up with the others

>And the rain continued to come down *(cue in rain)*
>and the animals all spoke at once. *(cue in animal noises, then kill the sound FX)*
>And everyone made a frightful racket.
>Then the rain got worse.

Cue in feet stamping

>And the boat rocked, and Noah and the animals rocked as well.

Lead a massive group sway, one way and then the other

>And it was all very frightening, BUT –

Cue in total silence

>Noah, and his family, and the animals were totally safe.
>They were very wet, but the boat protected them.

Ask the kids to sit down (where they are is fine)

> Does anyone know what Noah's boat was called?
> **(The Ark)**
> Quite right, the Ark.
> It's an odd name for a boat, because an ark usually looks like this –

Produce the chest

> A box, with a lid. The sort of box things can't fall out of.

Turn it upside down

> I think the boat was called the Ark because, as long as you were inside, you were safe.
> And when Christians read this story in the Bible, they thought, 'Hey, the Church is very like a ship – in fact, it's very like Noah's Ark.
> It's large – and safe – and you can't fall out, and it's going somewhere.
> Noah's Ark was making for dry land –
> where do you think the ship of the Church is going?

(See what they come up with, establish it's going to Heaven)

> And there's another similarity between the Church and the Ark – you enter it by getting very wet indeed.

Cue in Holy Baptism

Script 11 Candles
(The Presentation of Jesus in the Temple Script 1)
Luke 2.22–39 or Luke 2.22–33

> **THEME**
>
> This is an address for churches that use candles to celebrate Jesus' presentation in the Temple. Traditionally the candles are lit and blessed outside the church building,[31] then held in procession as priest and people enter the church for Mass – hence Candlemas. Simeon hails the Infant Jesus as 'A light to lighten the Gentiles'. Most churches are made up of Gentiles and this session considers the implications of Simeon's greeting. It also reminds us of the importance of the Jews in God's plan of salvation.[32] If you have any Christians of Jewish descent in your congregation see if they'd be prepared to come forward when you talk about the Chosen Race. Their presence will add greatly to the unravelling of this Gospel. Talking about 'Jew' and 'Gentile' is a potential minefield in the twenty-first century but, as the Bible is robust in its attitude to the various peoples of the earth, it seems sensible to tackle this aspect of Holy Scripture – adding modern sensitivity along the way.

GOSPEL   Luke 2.22–33

For a Family Eucharist the shorter version (Luke 2.22–33) is to be preferred. The Gospel is read in the usual way, and the congregation blow out their candles at the end.

---

31 The Procession re-enacts Jesus' first entrance into the Temple.

32 St Paul puts it very pithily: 'The Jew first, and then the Greek' (Romans 1.16). By 'Greek' Paul means 'Gentile'.

Script 11 – Candles (The Presentation of Jesus in the Temple Script 1)

SET UP

- A large map of the world. (Buying an upside-down map of the world – seen from an Australian perspective – provides a good springboard for the homily. Such maps could be bought online for £4.99 at the time of writing.)
- Somebody to hold up the map.
- Pictures 11.1–11.11 and the candle template from www.canterburypress.co.uk/downloads.
- A1 flip-chart to stick them to.
- Think through the various nationalities present in your congregation before the service. (Children are usually delighted to tell you about their ancestry – 'I'm a quarter French'. If you have a homogeneous congregation, home in on parts of the British Isles: Scotland, Yorkshire, Wales and so on.)

ADDRESS

Start off by showing the children the map of the world – ask somebody to hold it up as you'll need some flexibility when the kids come forward to point out the countries.

OPTIONAL START

If you've got an 'Australian' map of the world, start with that

> I'm going to start with this –

Your assistant holds up the map

> Can anyone tell me what it is?

There's often a baffled silence – eventually somebody will say

> **(It's a map …)**
> Excellent – but what's it a map of?

Tease it out of them, and wait for them to realize what's wrong

> **(It's a map of the world *and* it's upside down)**

Do a double take

> Good Heavens – you're right. It's an Australian map.
> Can anyone see England?

Get someone up to point it out

> Blimey, we're at the bottom!
> The Australians think we're the ones that are upside down.
> Fortunately, *Name (your assistant)* is on the case –

He/she turns it the right way up

MAP OF THE WORLD

> So here we are with a map of the world.
> Who's good at geography?
> Where's the UK?

Ask a child to come up and point it out

> How about Africa?

Another child (or adult) points this out

> Brilliant – anyone here come from an African country?

Acknowledge any hands that go up

Go through a few more countries, homing in on ones that members of the congregation have a connection with.[33] Leave the British subdivisions for the next section

> OK, well, way back when the world began, the world didn't look like this. It took some time for the countries to get in position – but they ended up like this eventually, and naturally the world filled up

THE PEOPLES OF THE WORLD

Move over to the flip-chart and stick on pictures of the peoples of the world as you mention them. They are anachronistically dressed – this session is about nations, not Palaeolithic man.

Don't use all the pictures; choose countries that reflect your congregation, and add some you can safely joke about (see below), and put in a few far-flung people like Laplanders. Make sure you include the Jews

Leave a gap in the middle of the pictures for Picture 11.11, which will be Jesus

Ad lib as you put up the pictures

> India filled up with Indians. (*Picture 11.1*)
> And China with the Chinese. (*Picture 11.2*)
> And right up in the really cold bit lived the Laplanders. (*Picture 11.3*)
> Then over in Europe we've got some very dodgy people –
> Who lived in Britain?
> **(The British)**

---

[33] We discovered that this part of the sermon had the unexpected benefit of giving newcomers a chance to make themselves known. Some Asians and Australians were delighted to wave their hands at the right moment.

Quite so. *(up goes Picture 11.4 of an Ancient Briton)*
Blimey, he needs a shave …
Up here in Norway lived the Vikings *(Picture 11.5)*
Golly, just as bad …
And what about Scotland?
(The Scottish)
Yup. *(Picture 11.6)*
He looks just like *Name (any local Scot who's up for it)* doesn't he?

Zip through a couple of other localities for Pictures 11.7, 11.8 and 11.9 *and end with …*

And over in Israel, lived the Jews. *(Picture 11.10)*
Now when the world started, God and all the people of the world seem to have got on.
Then something happened.
Nobody knows what.
But somehow people got the idea they could live without God, and they stopped praying and began to behave badly.
It was all very miserable.
And God looked down on His world and felt the lights had gone out.
He thought, 'I must put this right.'
So He decided He'd take one nation of the Earth and teach them what He was like. Just one nation, so He could do it quickly.
It was like being on the Fast Track. He looked round the world.
'Hmm,' He thought, 'which nation shall I choose?'
And He chose the Jews.[34] *(indicate Picture 11.10)*
So the Jews got to know God very well.
They were called the Chosen Race.
And all the other people in the world were called the Gentiles.
Have we got a member of the Chosen Race here?

Any person of Jewish descent is welcomed forward. Congratulate them on their heritage – what a privilege …

But what about the rest of us?
We're Gentiles.
God loves us just as much and, when He thought the Jews were ready, He sent His own Son to be born as a Jew and tell the world how much God loved them.

---

34 Sometimes children ask, 'Why the Jews?' There is no answer to this, perhaps it was they came from a civilized part of the world – or perhaps God liked their sense of humour.

Script 11 – Candles (The Presentation of Jesus in the Temple Script 1)

So Jesus came to Earth. (*Picture 11.11*)
And, when He was a little boy, His parents took Him to the Temple to be presented to God.
And there He met an old man, Simeon, who said, 'This child will be a light to lighten the Gentiles.'

Stick one of the candles, from the candle template, to Jesus' hand

Simeon knew that Baby Jesus would grow up and tell people about God and, because of Him, everyone in the world would eventually know how much God loved them.
It would be like putting the lights on again.
So Laplanders, Indians, Australians – even the British – heard the Good News.

As you mention these nationalities, stick candles on their pictures

That's why we've been carrying candles in church today.
Jesus' light has got as far as *Name (your locality)* and all of us, Jews and Gentiles, have come here to be lights in the world, and to thank God for Jesus.
Happy Candlemas!

Script 12 Christingle

(The Presentation of Jesus in the Temple Script 2)

Luke 2.22–33, 36–38

> **THEME**
>
> Many churches have a Christingle service during the Christmas season and, if you've managed to get to Candlemas without having one, here's the moment to catch up.[35] The Christingle is a German tradition from the Moravian Church and features an orange with a candle stuck in the top, surrounded by sweets. It's an appealing decoration and fits in neatly with Simeon's proclamation of Jesus as the Light of the World.

SET UP

- Materials for Christingle: orange, ribbon, cocktail sticks plus raisins, sultanas, glacé fruits or dolly mixture, four cloves.
- Make a couple of cuts in the orange before the service and make sure you can jam a small candle in the top.
- Matches.
- Cards for DIY Christingles (template for Christingle) and Pictures 12.1–12.5 from www.canterburypress.co.uk/downloads.

Optional

- Night light – tea light in a saucer, surrounded by water.
- Torch.

---

[35] Candlemas is absolutely the last day of Christmas.

Script 12 – Christingle (The Presentation of Jesus in the Temple Script 2)

PLACING THE GOSPEL

You can set up the Gospel with a story about light and dark (below) and then move into a homily after the Gospel, or you could ditch the first session and go straight into the sermon after the Gospel.

LIGHT AND DARK (OPTIONAL)

You need to set up the difference between dark and light. As your service will doubtless be held in broad daylight you will probably not be able to darken the church, so offer the children a story about the dark. If you've got a story about being left in the dark, or walking home in the dark, tell it now – and make sure it climaxes at the moment you found a torch. The one I use is this:

NIGHT LIGHTS

When I was very small my brother and I were frightened of the dark, so our parents gave us night lights. They were little candles, placed in a dish and surrounded by water.

Produce the night light and light it

It's nice, isn't it?
So this is me, with my night light.

(*Picture 12.1*) And my brother had one too. But one night I noticed his bit of the room was still dark.

(*Picture 12.2*) 'Christopher,' I said. 'What's happened to your light?'
'I've put it under my bed,' he said.

Look up with horror at this remark

Why was that really silly?
(Because it might catch light and burn something)
'WHY??!' I said.
'Because I'm frightened there're tigers under my bed, and now I'll be able to see them.' And at that moment a strange smell started to fill the room …

Draw in some wisps of smoke

Like burning.
We both rushed out of our beds and ran to the door, and the next moment our dad was in the room. He put out the fire at once – and after that Christopher and I were given …

Script 12 – Christingle (The Presentation of Jesus in the Temple Script 2)

Produce the torch

> a little torch.
> *(Look up)* Does anyone here understand torches?
> How do I switch it on?

Clock up the show of hands, and get a kid to show you how to switch it on. Talk about torch light – is it better than candlelight?

> Why don't we use torches instead of candles in our church?

(Take what comes, establish the fact that candles give a glowing light – not a beam, they look nice, and make other things look nice too)

> In fact, candles are not just useful, they are beautiful.
> It's a good thing to have beautiful things in a church, it reminds us that God made beautiful things – like babies, and light, and flame – and it's very important to have candles today, because it's Candlemas. That's the day when Baby Jesus was brought to the Temple for the first time, to be presented to God.

GOSPEL St Luke 2.22–33, 36–38

ADDRESS

> Let's go through that story. Jesus was brought by his parents …

Put up Picture 12.3 – Mary, Joseph and the Christ child; the children can probably tell you their names

> to the Temple, to be presented.
> The Jews thought that every firstborn son really belonged to God, and people should present their little boy to God – and buy him back.
> You got your son back for 5 shekels.
> Actually you didn't *have* to do it – but Mary and Joseph obviously took their faith seriously and they turned up with the money. You were also supposed to sacrifice something, a lamb or – if you were poor – two pigeons … Can you see what Joseph is carrying?
> Yep, two pigeons.
> When Jesus and His parents got to the Temple an old woman, Anna (*Picture 12.4*), thanked God for Baby Jesus, and an old man, Simeon (*Picture 12.5*), held out his arms to Jesus and said, 'This Child will be the Light of the world.'
> Why do you think he said that? *(this is probably a rhetorical question)*

It's because Jesus came into the world to sort out a mess. The world had gone wrong. People felt as if they were living in the dark. But Jesus came like a torch, or a candle, or a light bulb, to chase away the darkness and fill the world with light.

So today is Candlemas, and we carry candles to remember that Jesus is the Light of the World.

And we can make our own Candlemas candle at home, it's called a Christingle.

CHRISTINGLE

Make a large Christingle as a demo; you can dish out little Christingle cards at the end of the service so children can make them at home – adding clementines and candles etc. if your budget runs to it

> This orange is the world.
> It is surrounded by God's love.

Tie the ribbon round the middle

> The world is full of wonderful things, these are the fruits of the world –

Stick in cocktail sticks with the soft sweets or raisins

> God loved the world so much that He sent Jesus down to die for it –

Stick the four little cloves round the top (they represent the nails that crucified Christ)

> And He sent Jesus to be the Light of the World.

Stick in the candle and light it. Hold it up

> There you are, Jesus lighting the World.

OPTIONAL

> We'll have that burning on the altar *(place it)* as we get on with the rest of Candlemas.

Script 13 The Annunciation

Luke 1.26–38 (or Luke 1.26–32a, 34–35, 38)

> **THEME**
> We meet a courteous angel and learn to appreciate a very well-known phrase.

SET UP

The session requires the services of a colleague (cleric or lay) who has the self-possession to breeze in as the angel Gabriel. Angels are apparently neutral in gender, though Gabriel is always referred to as 'he'

Gabriel will need:
- A white alb and rope girdle.
- Some angel wings (Amazon have a good cheap selection).

Ask some adults to be ready to help with the various forms of greeting you'll find below

GOSPEL   Luke 1.26–38 – though the shorter version (Luke 1.26–32a, 34–35, 38) is better for this service

The homily is in two parts and frames the Gospel. The angel (if he or she is ordained) would be ideal as the Gospel reader.

Whoever reads the Gospel, make sure they say 'Hail, favoured one …' when Gabriel greets Our Lady (instead of the 'Greetings, favoured one' in the NRSV translation).

Script 13 – The Annunciation

ADDRESS Part 1

GREETINGS

>Good morning, everyone!

Acknowledge the response (if any) and beam at the congregation anyway

>Have you noticed how often we greet each other in church?
>If I say, 'The Lord be with you', what do you say?
>**(And with thy spirit/And also with you)**
>Of course on ordinary days I greet friends differently.
>If I see *Name (one of the children)* in the street,
>I say …

Wave a hand

>Hiya!
>And if I see *Name (a grown-up near you)*, I do this –

Shake him/her by the hand

>Good morning!
>Why do we shake hands?

(Kids normally say because it's polite, the traditional explanation is that it's to show you aren't holding a weapon.)

>It's polite. The old-fashioned word for politeness is 'courtesy'.

COURTESY

>We do a lot of odd things to be courteous.
>Sometimes we don't shake hands, sometimes we kiss each other like this –

Do a formal kiss with another grown-up, cheek to cheek × 2

>The French greet each other like that, but they do it three times.
>Bonjour!

Kiss your unfortunate friend again × 3

>And Parisians kiss each other *four* times.

You and your friend look at each other (ad lib)

>I think three's enough …
>The Chinese and Japanese don't kiss or shake hands. Do you know what they do?
>**(Bow)**
>Can you show me?

Place your hands flat on your thighs and exchange a short bow with the children

> Courtesy is the way people get on with one another. *(Everybody has a go at bowing)*

ROMAN COURTESY

> Back in Roman times they greeted each other like this –

Walk up to another adult, raise your hand, and say

> Ave, *Name*!

They respond in similar fashion

> 'Ave' is just Latin for 'Hail':
> I'll do that again in English.

Raise your hand and say to a member of the choir or a server

> Hail, *Name*!

He or she raises their hand and says 'Hail, Name!' back

> Can you do that?

Greet a child or two

> Hail, *Name*!

Then greet all of them, and raise your hand

> Hail, Children!

(With any luck they'll respond)

> Thank you, that's very courteous.
> Now I don't know what language they speak in Heaven –

Entrance of angel

Angel	*(marching down from the back)* I do!
Preacher	Good Heavens – this is a bit of a surprise –
Angel	*(raises his/her hand and greets you)* Hail, *Name*!
Preacher	Hail – um – have you got a name?
Angel	Yup, my name's Gabriel.
Preacher	*(raising hand)* Hail, Gabriel!

Ad lib the next bit, establish that our visitor is an angel. Check out the wings ...

Preacher	Are those real wings?
Angel	Of course!
Preacher	I mean, can you fly?
Angel	Naturally I can fly.

Script 13 – The Annunciation

Appears to take off and thinks better of it

        But not in an enclosed space – I might hit the – *(insert any well-known feature of your church, especially anything you've just had restored)*

Preacher   And what language *do* you speak in Heaven?

Angel   *(a chance to be regional here)* Welsh, of course! *(finish by saying):* But of course we all know Latin.
I learnt my manners from the Romans.

Preacher   Well, we're going to hear about Gabriel in today's Gospel; listen out for his greeting –

Straight into the **GOSPEL** *Luke 1.26–38 (or Luke 1.26–32a, 34–35, 38) (Gabriel greets Our Lady with a 'Hail! Favoured one!')*

ADDRESS Part 2

So today we heard that the angel Gabriel came down from Heaven and greeted a young woman called Mary.
What was the first thing he said?
(**'Hail, Favoured one!' 'Hail, Mary'** *if they don't come up with 'Hail Mary' add, 'perhaps Gabriel greeted her by name. What would he have said?')*
So, Gabriel was courteous. Then he gave Mary a message from God. Can anyone tell me what it was?
(**Mary was going to have a baby, she was going to have God's Son**)
Mary was going to be the Mother of God's Son.
Then, this is the interesting bit, Gabriel didn't zap off. He didn't say, 'Got that?' and leave. No, he waited.
There was a bit of a silence.
Because it wouldn't happen unless Mary agreed.

God is also very courteous. He doesn't just burst in and tell you what to do – He allows you to choose.
What did Mary say?
(**Yes/Let it be/Behold, the handmaid of the Lord**)
Could she have said 'No'? *(See what they think)*
She could have said 'No'.
I wouldn't be surprised if everything in Heaven went completely silent as God and the angels waited for her reply.
Fortunately, she said 'Yes' – and she became the Mother of Jesus.

So, let's kneel to thank Mary for her readiness to do God's will.
We'll do that in the prayer that uses Gabriel's greeting.

Pray the 'Hail Mary' together. If it's a prayer that your congregation is unfamiliar with, ask them to repeat the first part of the prayer after you

**Hail Mary,
Full of grace,
Blessed art thou amongst women
And blessed is the fruit of thy womb, Jesus,
Amen**[36]

---

36 Don't try to 'sell' the 'Hail, Mary'. If you're asked about it after the service you may find it helpful to deconstruct the prayer. It is made of two Gospel phrases, one taken from the angel Gabriel and the other from Mary's cousin, Elizabeth. The complete prayer finishes with a request that Our Lady will pray for us at the hour of our death – as she did at the foot of the Cross.

Script 14 Ash Wednesday

Matthew 6.1–18

> **THEME**
>
> Ash Wednesday is the one day of the year when it is meritorious to have a dirty face and, given that children usually like being ashed, you may wish to transfer the Ash Wednesday rite to a family service at the beginning of Lent. It's helpful if the sermon, the Gospel and the ashing run as one continuous whole. That way, Jesus' strictures on not showing off and the ashing proper will be seen to complement each other.

SET UP

- A1 flip-chart with 7 pre-drawn faces (and 4 template faces) from www.canterburypress.co.uk/downloads. Faces 1–3 to be on sheet 1 as: female unhappy, male happy and male unhappy. Faces 4–7 to be on sheet 2 as: male happy, male unhappy, female unhappy and female happy. Face 4 should already be marked up with a St George Cross. See 14.1–14.7 templates for the expressions to draw on the faces.
- Three bullet-tipped marker pens in black, red and blue.
- At the very beginning of the service introduce the season of Lent. It would slow things up to explain 'Lent' in the homily.

GOSPEL

Follows the ADDRESS, move into it as naturally as your rite allows.

ADDRESS

Straight to the flip-chart

>> OK, today I'm going to talk about face painting.
>> Has anyone ever had their face painted?

Register the show of hands and ask one kid for details. Include the others in the answer with an ad lib: anyone else been painted to look like a tiger?

Actors (*Picture 14.1 template*)

> Well, grown-ups paint their faces too.
> Actors do it to look old –

Add frown and worry lines to the face (these and all subsequent marks are shown on the template)

Clowns (*Picture 14.2 template*)

> Clowns do it to look funny.
> Can anyone here show me what a clown puts on his face?

Hand the red pen over to someone – they should be able to manage the red nose, possibly even the cheek pattern (see template)

Ancient Britons (*Picture 14.3 template*)

> Sometimes people put paint on their face to look fierce.
> The Ancient Britons used to wear war paint.

Add blue war paint to the face

> Those swirly lines were painted on with a blue dye called woad.
> And, right now, modern Britons put paint on their faces –

Turn the next page of the flip-chart

St George's Cross (*Picture 14.4 template*)

> What sort of grown-up marks his face like this?
> **(An England supporter, a football fan)**
> Quite right – but why does he choose a cross?

Establish that the red cross is the symbol of St George and the flag of England. (If you've got a Union Jack in church you could point it out among the other crosses.)

> Why do you suppose St George has the cross as his symbol?

*This might be rhetorical; establish that St George has the cross **because he's a Christian***

> The cross is the badge of the Christian.
> OK, hang on to that and let's look at this chap –

Script 14 – Ash Wednesday

Roman (*Picture 14.5 template*)

> This man is a Roman. Romans did *not* mark their faces. They were very neat and tidy, clipped their hair short, and shaved their chins – *except* when somebody died.
> When that happened, the Romans would stop brushing their hair *(add a few strokes to make the hair look unkempt)*,
> stop shaving *(add stubble)*, and smeared ash all over their faces. *(add a few strokes of ash to the forehead)*
> There, what a mess.
> Anybody looking at him would know he was really unhappy.
> Well, when Roman Christians wanted to look unhappy,
> they'd do the same thing – why *would* a Christian be unhappy?

The kids may well say that Christians are unhappy when people die

> Yup, though actually Roman Christians weren't quite as unhappy as ordinary Romans, because they knew that the dead went to Heaven.

(Take what comes, and move on to the idea that …)

> Christians are only really unhappy when they remember their sins – all the stupid things they've done.
> So, at the beginning of Lent, Christians mark their faces with ash – just like the Romans – to show they are sorry.
> But, as they are Christians, they make the sign of the cross.

Add an ash cross to the forehead of the **Christian** (*Pictures 14.6 template*)

> So, there's a Christian, very sorry for all the sins he has committed.
> But, guys, are Christians really unhappy people?
> (**No!**)
> No, they're not – because Christians know that when they are sorry for their sins God will forgive them at once. (*Picture 14.7 template*)
> So, though, we come to church today (Ash Wednesday) to say sorry, and put on ash to *show* we are sorry; we go home and wash our faces at once, because we know God has forgiven us.
> Let's hear what Jesus says about how He'd like Christians to behave in Lent, and then we'll kneel at the altar to receive the ash cross on our foreheads.

Straight into

GOSPEL Matthew 6.1–18

Make a slight gesture, from hand to hand, when you read the passage about the left not knowing what the right is doing, and lighten up the text a bit.

POSSIBLE PARAPHRASE OF THE GOSPEL

> Jesus said: 'Whenever you do good, try not to show off. If you give money away, don't blow a trumpet about it – so everyone will know how good you are. No, when you give to the poor, make sure your left hand doesn't know what your right hand is doing. Give your money secretly, and your Father – who sees in secret – will reward you.
> And when you pray, don't act at being good. That's what the hypocrites do, praying out loud, and making sure everyone knows they go to church. Well, they have had their reward. When you pray, go into your room, close the door, and pray to your Father in secret, and your Father – who sees in secret – will reward you.
> And when you fast, don't look miserable like the hypocrites. They put stuff on their faces so everyone knows they are fasting – but don't copy them. When you fast, tidy up, wash your face, and fast in secret. And your Father – who sees in secret – will reward you.

Script 15   Lent 1

(A) Matthew 4.1–11
(B) Mark 1.12–13
(C) Luke 4.1–13

> **THEME**
>
> This can be used for any service about Lent. The address is more about the season than a specific passage of Scripture. The seriousness of the Lenten readings will set the scene as you consider Lent as a time of preparation. How do we prepare for things? Well, by getting the right kit, or putting on special clothes – or by stripping back …

SET UP

- Flag up the change of liturgical colour from green to purple on the altar frontal and the vestments. If you're stuck, drape a purple cloth over the front of the lectern.
- Emphasize the pared-down nature of Lent. Perhaps your church removes the flowers, or doesn't play incidental music (like the Voluntary)? Others cut down the number of times a bell is rung.[37] No Alleluias are said or sung in Lent, nor is the Gloria.
- Set up the kit for
  - a diver
  - a climber
  - a cyclist
  - motorcyclist
  - anything that requires distinctive clothes and exciting extras (like coils of rope or a large helmet).
- A stick of white, or brightly coloured, sun block from the local sports shop.
- Swimming trunks.

---

[37] Very old-fashioned Catholics use rattles (like old-fashioned football rattles) instead of bells, children love them.

- Put all this kit into a large cardboard box – the swimming trunks at the bottom.
- A stooge ready to give you a hand; he – it works better with a chap – should be wearing an easily removable top garment.
- A purple stole.
- A purple veil or cloth.
- Some ashes left over from Ash Wednesday, moisten them before the service.
- If the preacher is one of the clergy it looks effective to preach in a simple alb, reserving your purple garments for later.

ADDRESS

GETTING UP

Greet the children – and congratulate them for being in church

> Does anyone remember getting up this morning?

React to the forest of hands

> Gosh, all of you?
> Right, well you started in bed – and now you're here in church.
> What happened? Did you just jump out of bed and walk down the road?

The children will be anxious to tell you that they got dressed, had breakfast, got in the car – whatever

> OK, I understand – you got ready for church.

GETTING READY

> Actually, we're always getting ready for things: going to school, going on holiday – and it usually means sorting out some kit.
> Supposing I was going to climb a mountain?
> What sort of things do you think I'd need?

Take a couple of answers, but keep it moving as you bring the cardboard box forward

> OK, well let's see what we've got here. Who'd like to be kitted up as a mountaineer?

You and the volunteer pull the mountaineering kit out of the box. Keep a patter going as the kid puts things on (it doesn't matter if they don't fit very well)

> How about an anorak? Yup, it's cold up there.
> And a rucksack with your lunch inside?
> And a safety helmet? *(a cycling helmet will do)*

Script 15 – Lent 1

> And some gloves
> And, most important – yup, some rope! *(drape this over one shoulder)*
> Brilliant!
> See you at the top of Everest!

Ask the child to stand to one side

> How about cycling?

Get another kid up and talk him/her through putting on a cycling helmet, a visibility jacket/belt, cycle clips – anything you've got. (A motor cycling helmet and gloves would go down very well)

Admire the two kids

> Yup, they look ready for anything.
> Actually, sometimes we need to put things on our faces to get ready.
> What do we put on our faces if we're going to run round in the sun?
> **(Suntan lotion/sun block)**

Hold up sun block

> Even skiers need stuff on their faces – the sun is very fierce in the mountains. Anyone want to try this?

Anoint a volunteer – mark their faces very deliberately as you tell the kids that the bits that need protecting are the ridges on the face – the cheek bones, the ears and the nose. (This is always very popular)

Admire the result

> The sun block has to be a really obvious colour, so the skier knows if it's got rubbed off.

This child too stands aside

> But sometimes you need to take things off to get ready.
> How about swimming?
> Would anyone like to show how we get ready for swimming?

The stooge comes forward

> OK, what do you need to go swimming?

Look at him

> Well, you can't wear that jacket for a start.
> What else has to go?

He takes off anything else that is feasible

> Gosh, your shirt as well –

Pull out the trunks

> Are these worn over your jeans?
> No?

Stooge offers to take off his trousers

> Stop there! We get the idea!
> So these guys put things *on* to get ready.
> This kid puts stuff on her face to get ready.
> And this guy takes things *off* to get ready.
> And we do just the same in church.

GETTING READY FOR EASTER

> This is the time of year when the church gets ready for Easter.
> It takes us six weeks, and those six weeks are called Lent.
> In Lent we put some things on – priests, for example, start wearing purple …

Pull out a purple stole and/or chasuble and put it on – or ask one of the clergy to come forward with these garments on

> And at the beginning of Lent we mark our faces.
> We did that on Ash Wednesday.
> Can anyone remember what we do on that day?

Throw this open to everyone, somebody will know

> Yes, we put ash on our faces.
> Would anyone like to be ashed?

Mark the child with an ash cross

> We do this for lots of reasons; one of them is to remember that Jesus died on the cross.
> But most of the time in Lent, we get rid of things.

Go with local custom here

> No extra music, no flowers, no bells, no Gloria, no cheery hymns with Alleluia! in them.
> Everything becomes very simple and plain.
> Eventually we even cover up the statues – like this …

Script 15 – Lent 1

Ask a child to come up, stand as still as a statue, then throw a purple veil over them

> Yup, we won't be seeing *Name* now until Easter Day.

Take the purple veil off

> So that's Lent.

Ask the stooge quickly and quietly to put the kit away as you wrap up. If you can, mark the change of mood by sitting down with the kids, in an obvious 'let's think about this' gesture

> Why do you think we do this?

Take all answers – but keep it moving

> Well, Lent is a serious time and purple is a dark serious colour.
> The ash reminds us of the Cross Jesus died on.
> And not having lots of cheerful things in church helps us to be serious and quiet.
> We can think about all the things that happened during the first Easter.
> And I'll tell you something, if you've been serious for a bit, it's marvellous when you think, OK, I'm glad it's been quiet, but now it's time to lighten up.
> Like right now!
> There you are – sitting in front of me, looking serious.
> Now it's time to … *(collectively catch their eye)*
> Get ready –
> Watch me –
> OK –
> JUMP UP!

The kids do

> Brilliant!
> Just sit down again for a second.

To the adults

> The children have just given us a foretaste of Easter.
> We've got six weeks of Lent ahead of us – but at the end of it is Easter Day, and that's the moment when Jesus Himself …
> OK, kids – are you ready?
> JUMPS UP!

Up they jump again – send them back to their seats.

Script 16   The Transfiguration[38]

(A) St Matthew 17.1–8
(B) Lent 2 Roman Catholic: Mark 9.2–9 or
Sunday before Lent C of E: Mark 8.31–34
(C) Luke 9.28–36

> **THEME**
>
> **The session is about transformation – the absolutely normal transformation of something growing, changing, developing. We're used to it, but of course it usually happens quite slowly. Jesus didn't need to develop, He already was the Son of God, and – as He prayed on the Mount of Transfiguration – His real nature shone through.**

SET UP

- A transformer toy – I suppose it's useless to hope there's one on the market that doesn't turn into a gun-toting robot; the kids won't be bothered anyway.
- A1 flip-chart, marker pens – black and yellow.
- Pictures 16.1–16.10 from www.canterburypress.co.uk/downloads. First you'll need the pictures of things being transformed (they're very easy, you might want to follow the template and draw them yourself). The Transfiguration pictures come next; make sure they are covered before you start the story.
- Three kids prepared to be Peter, James and John.
- A biscuit tin, a toy drum, piece of tinplate – anything you can use for thunder – plus someone to produce the effect on cue.

ADDRESS

Start off with a transformer toy

>   Does anyone know what this is?

(They all will)

---

38 The Transfiguration turns up, for both Anglicans and Roman Catholics, in the weeks before Easter, but at slightly different times. There is a separate Feast of the Transfiguration on August 6th.

Script 16 – The Transfiguration

> So how does it work?

Select a kid who can be trusted to turn it into something else at speed. Admire the robot or whatever it is

> That's clever – does it go back?

Ask another kid to restore it

> Amazing!
> Jesus liked transformations – not toys, real things.

Change the following pictures, using the template. (They are so easy you could probably draw them neatly and cover yourself with glory)

(*Pictures 16.1*) He liked seeds turning into plants – that takes ages.
(*Picture 16.2 & 16.3*) Or a sick person getting better – Jesus could do that very fast.
(*Picture 16.4 & 16.5*) Or a bad guy becoming good.

> And there was one day when Jesus Himself was transformed.
> It was completely natural – like us turning into saints – but it happened rather quickly, and it frightened His friends to bits.
> Let's think about the Gospel story again …

Move across to the flip-chart, hold up the picture of Jesus looking 'normal'

(*Picture 16.6*) Here's a picture of how Jesus looked as He walked round the countryside telling people about God.
> He did that for a couple of years, but He knew He had to go to Jerusalem, the capital of the Holy Land, and teach there.
> It was very dangerous, but Jesus was determined to do the job His Father had given Him properly.

Give the Jesus picture to a helper; you'll need it later

> But first He went away to pray to God His Father – and He took some friends. They were Peter, James and John.

Ask your previously cast kids down the front

> Anyone else like to be Jesus' mates?

Add any child who wants to help; it may be all of them

> So Jesus, and Peter and James and John, climbed a mountain. And Jesus went to the very top as Peter, James and John knelt to pray.

The kids kneel

> When suddenly it was as if a curtain had gone up.
> Jesus looked completely different.

Remove the cover over picture 16.7 and point out the details as you tell the story

> His face shone,
> His clothes became dazzling white, and

> He stood there talking to some great heroes, whom the disciples thought were dead – Moses and Elijah. (*Pictures 16.8 & 16.9*)
> Peter and James and John jumped up.

The kids jump up

> There was a mighty crack of thunder

Thunder effect

> and they heard God Himself telling them that Jesus was His Beloved Son. Peter, James and John fell flat on their faces.

The kids do just that

> Then suddenly, it was all OK – the thunder stopped,
> Moses and Elijah disappeared *(turn over to the next blank sheet)* and the disciples sat down – very quietly.

The kids sit round you

> And Jesus was looking normal again.

Stick up the 'normal' Jesus (Picture 16.6)

> Peter said, 'Shall we make some huts and stay here, Lord?'
> 'No,' said Jesus. 'We must get on to Jerusalem.'

Make a slight break and come centre stage

> What was all that about?
> I think it's about Jesus making a decision: He was going to go to Jerusalem and get on with the next bit of the job. He was the Son of God, and for a moment He *looked* like the Son of God.
> He was *transfigured*.
> But Jesus couldn't hang around on that mountain, He moved on

Depending on when you celebrate the Feast of the Transfiguration (the Sunday next before Lent, or Lent 2), wrap this up by saying

> and we've got to move on with Jesus, as we start our Lenten journey next Wednesday towards Easter.

or

> And we've got to move on with Jesus, as we continue our Lenten journey to Holy Week.

> Because we are being transfigured as well – it will take a bit of time. But one day *(reveal Pictures 16.10 of a group of kids)* we will look like the people we really are, deep down –

Add yellow rays of light round the kids

> And, that is – saints!

Script 17   Mothering Sunday

(Lent 4 Script 1)
(Using the Gospel of the Prodigal Son)

St Luke 15.11b–32

> **THEME**
>
> It might seem odd that the Prodigal Son, with its all-male cast, is one of the Gospels for Mothering Sunday, but there aren't many parent/child stories in the Gospels and few have a starring role for the mother.[39] Why that should be is the springboard for this homily. First-century Palestine was full of culturally 'invisible' women, and even in church this morning we have lots of 'invisible' mothers, in among the ones obviously present in the pews. Fortunately, we can thank God for all of them at the altar.

SET UP

- Children and adults prepared to play the very simple roles of Dad, Mum, the Prodigal Son, and the Elder Brother. This is one of the few occasions when you need boys to play boys and girls to play girls. You will need a very swift run-through.
- If you have a couple of willing actors in the congregation, you can ask them to ad lib the exchange between Mum and Dad (see below).
- See if anyone in the congregation will be prepared to acknowledge an absent mother by raising their hand. Obviously you'll know if this is a sensitive issue (somebody may have lost their mother recently), so adjust the script accordingly.

GOSPEL   St Luke 15.11b–32

---

[39] Apart from Jesus' parents of course, and the wonderfully ambitious mother of James and John.

ADDRESS

THE PRODIGAL SON

> Today we heard Jesus' story about a father

The father stands at the front

> who had two sons.
> The elder was a serious hard-working chap –

The elder brother joins his dad

> I've always thought he was called Reuben …
> while the younger – Junior – was happy-go-lucky, and incredibly thoughtless.

The younger son, the Prodigal, joins the other two

> Well, the younger son had the cheek to ask his father to give him all the money he'd get when his father died.

Dad hands over his wallet

> Then he ran off.

He does – right down to the end of the church

> There he goes.
> And he spent the whole lot and got into big trouble.
> Then he had to come home.

The boy returns very slowly – looking hangdog

> And his dad saw him, looking totally miserable, and he couldn't bear it. So he ran to greet him

Dad does so

> and brought him home,

Brings the boy up to the front, gets the wallet back (it's empty), pulls a face – then says, 'Oh, what the heck?'

> and forgave him.

The father puts his hand on the Prodigal's shoulder

> Reuben was not so pleased.

Reuben folds his arms – but eventually shakes hands when prompted by Dad

> And they sat down and had a feast – fatted calf, chips, ice cream – the lot!

WRAPPING UP THE STORY

> That's a great story.
> It's good to know that God, our Father, loves us, just like the dad in the story – and forgives us, whatever we do.

INVISIBLE WOMEN

> But, just a minute – there's something odd about this story.

Stand back from the cast

> Let's look at it, one father, two sons –
> Does anything strike you?

It probably will – give them a hand if they need it

> Didn't the boy have a mother?
> Who cooked the fatted calf they had for supper?

Enter the mother

> Ah, I thought so –
> You can just imagine it, can't you?

Dad	Hey! Junior's come back!
Mum	*(ruffling his hair or something)* So I see.
Dad	We're going to have a feast!
Mum	We are?
Dad	Yup – we're going to have a fatted calf!
Mum *(ad lib)*	Abe! What are you talking about? Fatted calf!? *What* fatted calf? What do you think we've got in the fridge? We're having gefilte fish for supper …!
Dad *(ad lib)*	Oh, come on, love, he's back. I'll nip down to the supermarket –
Mum	OK, hurry up –

Mum hugs Prodigal – meanwhile Dad has discovered he hasn't got any money: Mum hands over her purse with an expressive look

Dad	Thanks, love!
Preacher	So we've got Mum, and Dad, and two boys – and hey, what about his little sister? Anyone like to be the sister?

Get a child to join the line-up

> And his auntie

Add an adult

> and his gran.

Add another adult – stand back to admire the line-up

> That's more like it!
> So, *why* weren't there any girls in the story?
> Well, in the time when Jesus lived, it wasn't thought polite to mention women.
> Everyone knew they were there of course, but you didn't talk about them. It was as if they were invisible.

The girls exit

> They're just not there.

Turn to the chaps

> Actually, guys, you can exit too. Thanks!

VISIBLE MOTHERS

> That's an important thing to think about today, because it's Mothering Sunday.
> There are lots of mums in this church, and they are very visible indeed.
> Let's see how many mums we've got here??

Encourage them to wave

> It's super to come to church with your mother on Mothering Sunday.
> But she might not be sitting in the pew.

INVISIBLE MOTHERS

> You might have brought her in your heart.
> Because some people haven't got their mums with them – perhaps she couldn't make it, or perhaps she's died and is in Heaven with Jesus and Mary.

See if any people who haven't got their mums physically present will be prepared to put up a hand

> This morning, we've got a church full of mothers – visible and invisible – but all deeply loved.
> And when you kneel at the altar today I think it would be a good idea to bring your mother with you, whether you can see her or not, and thank God for her in your heart.

Script 18   Mothering Sunday
(Lent 4 Script 2)

This script can be used with any of the Mothering Sunday Gospels.

> **JESUS' FAMILY**
>
> Jesus came from a large family. Four brothers – James, Simon, Joses and Jude – are recorded in the Gospels, plus an unspecified number of sisters. The 'brothers and sisters' of Jesus, referred to in Matthew 12.46, Luke 8.19 and Mark 3.31, can easily be understood as wider kindred, or simply those he grew up with.[40] This extended use of 'brother' and 'sister' is still common in the Middle East and many other parts of the world. People noticed Jesus' Galilean accent when they met Him and, in Nazareth, He was known as 'Joseph's son', 'the carpenter's son' and the 'son of Mary'.[41] In other words, everybody thought that Jesus was 'ordinary' – He had a definable background and was brought up like everyone else. This address roots Jesus in His family and homes in the abiding presence of His mother, the Virgin Mary.

SET UP

- Pictures 8.1–8.12 (and templates 18.6a–18.6e) from www.canterburypress.co.uk/downloads. Note: six copies of Picture 18.3 are needed.
- A1 flip-chart.
- Marker pen.
- Put up the faces surrounding Jesus in the numbered sequence indicated below. The pictures of Mary's face are all blank. Look them up on the template and pencil them in beforehand – they're very easy and you will be able to draw them as you preach.

---

[40] See Script 7, The Holy Family, for a note on the perpetual virginity of Our Lady.
[41] An odd title. Jews were not usually called after their mother.

ADDRESS

Ad lib greetings to kids and their families

> Today is about families – our own family, the Church family, and our family in Heaven.
> But let's start with Jesus' family –
> When Baby Jesus first opened His eyes, He must have thought He had been born into a very odd family.
> The first things he saw were an ox and an ass (*Picture 18.1*).
> He saw His step-father, Joseph (*Picture 18.2*), and His mother, Mary (*Picture 18.3*).
> She was smiling. *(add a smile)*
> As Jesus got bigger, He found He had four brothers (*Picture 18.4*) – James, Simon, Joses and Jude – and so many sisters nobody seemed to know their names (*Picture 18.5*). And of course His mother (*Picture 18.3*). Though, given Jesus was a kid, His mother sometimes had the look on her face that I expect you know from your own mother –

Add wary expression to a new Picture 18.3 from template 18.6a

> You can imagine the sort of things Mary sometimes said to Him:
> 'Hey! What about tidying up your bedroom?'

Ad lib 'Life of Brian' remarks, if you think your congregation can cope

> 'You may be the Messiah, but you've still got to finish your chicken soup …' (*new Picture 18.3 with expression from template 18.6b*)
> 'Even Messiahs have to brush their hair –' (*new Picture 18.3 with expression from template 18.6c*)
> Then Jesus grew up, and He met all sorts of people.
> Children and fishermen, and people who liked Him and people who didn't and of course His Mum.
> Quite often she was giving Him advice and instructions, like –

Add the expression that accompanies the following remarks

> 'Jesus, they've run out of wine –' (*new Picture 18.3 with expression from template 18.6d*)
> 'Come home, Jesus!' (*new Picture 18.3 with expression from template 18.6e*)
> But she never stopped loving Him.
> But eventually the people who didn't like Jesus managed to get Him arrested and nailed Him to the Cross.

That was terrible – but as Jesus looked down from the Cross who did He see?

The soldiers who had put Him there, obviously – and His enemies – but also His best friend, John – and His mother (*Picture 18.7*).

She's looking quite old now *(add the lines)*, but she stayed with Him until the end.

But, as we all know, Jesus didn't remain dead: He rose on the third day – and *then* He saw His friends, Mary Magdalene, Peter – and His mother (*Picture 18.8*).

And now Jesus is in Heaven and, as He looks round, He sees loads of people. His family, and the friends He made on Earth, let's put in Peter (*Picture 18.9*) and the friends He's made since – my Granny (*Picture 18.10*), for example.

Choose any name that will go with the elderly face provided

and His mother (*Picture 18.11*).

Now Mary is the Queen of Heaven – *(add in a crown, Picture 18.12)*, but more than that, she's near her Son and she still loves Him.

Add smile to Mary's face

Who else does Jesus see in Heaven?

See if the kids want to add some names, saints, grandparents (not too many)

So there's Jesus with Mary and Peter and *Name* and *Name* and *Name*. And they – and we – are all His family, because He told us we have the same Heavenly Father.

Hang on to that as you go back to your seats – and remember how pleased Jesus will be when it's time for us to say the Family Prayer of the Church today, the 'Our Father'.

Script 19   Holy Week

> **THEME**
>
> Holy Week is so liturgically rich that it seems unlikely a traditional church would have time for a dedicated Family Eucharist, except on Easter Day itself. But that doesn't mean that children can't participate in the Great Week, and a variety of services and activities are offered below, ending with four Easter homilies for the family service.

PASSOVER

The Passover is at the heart of the first Holy Week. It's a great family meal and works well celebrated on the Saturday before Palm Sunday, so as not to clash with school or the major services ahead. Jewish people are excellent at home religion, and very generous about Gentiles joining them in celebrating their escape from Egypt. Passover is not like a church service, it's a family meal. A Jewish family says Passover together as they eat round the table – and the parents often throw in jokes and games to keep the children awake. You can find various Passovers for families online, and a simple one for young children is provided in *Creative Ideas for Children's Worship: Year B*, Script 50, 'The Last Supper' (Canterbury Press, 2012).

PALM SUNDAY

Palm Sunday marks the start of Holy Week and the Mass for that day doesn't give you much scope for a kids' homily, though the children will enjoy the blessing of the palms and the open-air procession into the church building. After that it's best to get them off to Children's Church while the adults participate in the Solemn Narration of the Passion. *Creative Ideas for Children's Worship Years A, B and C* give you a range of stories and activities centring on the Procession, the palms, the donkey, and the Passion itself.

GOOD FRIDAY

You can find children's versions of the Stations of the Cross and the Solemn Liturgy online. The *Stations* is designed for young children and avoids any graphic account of Jesus' suffering (small children are, naturally, distressed by the Eleventh Station – Jesus is nailed to the Cross); the *Solemn Liturgy* is for older children. Both services are interactive and come with set-up instructions, and a booklet you can print out.

THE EASTER GARDEN

Making an Easter Garden on Holy Saturday means the kids can join the musicians, flower arrangers and brass cleaners as they prepare the church for Easter. (Run this idea past these august groups first.) Instructions for making an Easter Garden can be found on many sites online.

EASTER DAY

Given the splendour of the Easter Vigil, you can safely ease up on Easter Day and welcome families and children to a joyful Easter Eucharist. It is astonishing how easily the ceremonies of High Mass accommodate themselves to a kids' sermon, egg rolling, and hand bells in the last hymn. So don't stint on the lace, the gold brocade, or the incense.

Script 20 Finding Jesus

(Easter Day Script 1)

Any Gospel that features the empty Tomb

THEME

An Easter homily for small children – finding Jesus is (almost) as exciting as looking for Easter Eggs.

SET UP

- Pictures 20.1–20.6. Four copies of Picture 20.3a are needed, three to be revealed with Pictures 20.4–20.6.
- A1 flip-chart top display pictures on.
- An Easter Egg in a presentation box – make sure it's hollow.
- Two or three very small eggs hidden in rather obvious places near you.
- A couple of helpful children or servers (see below). One of them has a picture of Jesus about her person.

ADDRESS

FINDING EGGS

       Happy Easter, everyone!
       I love this Sunday – what's one of the really nice things about Easter?

(Take all answers, reward piety, but home in on the kid who says **'Easter Eggs!'** *Make sure a server is ready to say this if the kids don't)*

       I got an Easter Egg this morning.

Produce the large egg – hold it up

       It's nice, isn't it?
       Do you know what the most important part of an Easter Egg is? Is it the cardboard box?
       (**No**)

OK, let's get rid of that. *(Do so)*
Oh, is it the nice ribbon?
(**No**)
Right, get rid of that ...
How about the foil?
(**No**)
OK, that's going ...
What about the chocolate – is it that?
(**Yes!**)
NO, it isn't. The chocolate is completely in the way – can anyone help me get rid of some of it?

Break the top off the egg, you want a substantial bit left.
Hand out some of the broken bits to the children, and hold the broken egg up

There you are, that's the important bit of an Easter Egg – that nice empty inside, there's nothing there!
That's the first message of Easter morning. We've just heard it in the Gospel.

THE EMPTY TOMB

Over to the flip-chart

On the very first Easter morning, three women got up early to find a friend. They were Mary the mother of Jesus, Mary Magdalene and Salome.
Their friend was dead, and they wanted to anoint His body and say goodbye to Him properly. So they went to His Tomb –

Reveal Pictures 20.1a and 20.1b of the Tomb, with the stone Blu-Tacked on in front of the opening

In those days people were often buried in caves.
Do you know who was buried in this one?
(**Jesus**)
Exactly.
Jesus had been placed there after He had died on the Cross.
His friends had laid Him inside, and rolled a huge stone in front of the doorway.

Point out the huge stone in front of the opening

And it wasn't until they got to the Tomb that the women began to worry about the stone – how were they going to move it?

But when they got nearer
they found the stone had been moved

One of the servers removes it

and that the Tomb was

Get the kids to look

Empty!
The women were horrified – where had Jesus gone? Then they noticed a young man in white

Stick on Picture 20.2 of the angel

standing beside the Tomb.
He said, 'What are you doing? Why are you looking for Jesus in a tomb? He's not here – He's alive! He's risen, just as He said He would!'

Well, that's pretty good news. The Tomb is empty – just like the Easter Egg.
But where's Jesus? One of the women saw Him …

Put on Picture 20.3a of Jesus with a detachable hat (Picture 20.3b)

and thought He was the gardener.
Then He said her name.
'Mary!'
And she realized who he was.

Take off the hat

So, the first Easter Day Jesus' friends had to look out for Him and recognize Him.
It's one of the reasons we look for eggs at Easter. There's a couple hidden round here – can you find them?

It should take a couple of seconds

Brilliant.
Well, Jesus didn't stay on Earth for ever – eventually He went back to Heaven.

Waft the Jesus picture off to Heaven

But before He went, He said He'd always be around for His friends.
And so He is, we just have to find Him.
He's in this church this morning.
Where do you suppose He is – behind the easel?
(**Nope**)

Under the piano? *(Nothing there)*
In the pews?

Get the kids to turn round and look at the adults

I can't see anyone there who looks remotely like Jesus.
We'll have to try harder. God said He can always be found if you look hard enough …

Pictures 20.4–20.6 of some church props, the Bible, chalice and host. Each picture has a cut out flap which conceals a picture of Jesus

Let's use our brains, and open this book – the Holy Bible.

Get a kid to open the flap

Aha! There's Jesus, of course – still speaking to us in the Gospel.
And what about the bread and the wine?

Open them

There He is again – He told us He'd always be present in the Bread and Wine at Mass.
And He's somewhere else. You can find out by giving each other the Peace.

You and the servers offer the Peace to the kids

There – every time I shook hands with one of you, I shook hands with Jesus. Jesus is in the hearts of His faithful people – even in young *Name* here …

Turn to the server

	Have you got Jesus in your heart, *Name*?
Server	I certainly have!
Preacher	How do you know?
Server	Look!

Pulls out the picture of Jesus

Brilliant! Jesus is alive. He's alive in our church this morning, in the Bible, in the Bread and Wine, and in the hearts of His people. Have a super Easter, enjoy your eggs when you get home, and remember to look out for Jesus. Because He's there to be found.

Script 21 The Paschal Candle

(Easter Day Script 2)

Any of the Easter Gospels.

THEME

A session for older children on Jesus: the Beginning and the End. It involves making a paschal candle together, with the help of the actual Paschal Candle, and you'll find the adults will be as fascinated as the kids in its symbolic marks and pins.

SET UP

- A chunky free-standing candle. Chose a good size but not as large as the actual Paschal Candle: this is the child-friendly version.
- Five mapping pins. If you find a pack of shiny ones, try to get one with five gold pins – brightly coloured ones are fine.
- Stick the pins in the candle before the session (see the Paschal Candle template from www.canterburypress.co.uk/downloads) and then remove them. It will make them much easier to insert during the homily.
- Red, blue and green marker pens that make a mark on wax – try them out first.
- Small table to put your props on.
- A taper.
- A fairy story, Cinderella for preference; make sure it is topped and tailed with the traditional 'Once upon a time' and 'They lived happily ever after'.
- A Bible; put a marker in Luke 2, and another at the end of John's Gospel.
- If your church uses incense, ensure the real Paschal Candle is censed at the same time as the priest censes the altar at the beginning of the service.

ADDRESS

BEGINNINGS AND ENDINGS

Ad lib a 'Happy Easter' as you take a seat and sit by the prop table (unless your church is so large you'd disappear from sight)

> I'm going to talk about stories today.
> I think it's interesting to see how they begin and end.
> Look, here's the story of – *(check it out)* – 'Cinderella' –
> Can anyone guess how that story will start?
> **(Once upon a time)**
> Let's see if you're right –

Refer to the book

> Yes, you're exactly right – 'Once upon a time'. I wonder when that was?

Not a serious question

> Nobody knows –

Riffle through the book

> Well, it all seems very exciting – Cinderella goes to a ball, and finds her prince, and – oo-er – loses her slipper, and the Prince has to find her.

Look up

> Does anyone know what happens then?

The children will tell you

> So everything's OK. Does anyone know the words that finish off this story?

(Be prepared for a child to say 'The End!' If that happens, grin – the congregation will certainly chuckle)

> Good one! OK – what about the words just before then?

You will get the proper formula eventually. Refer to the book

> 'They all lived happily ever after. The End.'
> Excellent. Now, when does the story of Jesus begin?

Keep this rhetorical, you haven't time for a wide-ranging discussion

> I happen to know this.

Refer to the Bible

> I've got it here. 'At the time when the Emperor Augustus ordered a census, when Quirinius was governor of Syria …'
> Gosh, when was that?

Apparently look at some footnotes

> Oh, anytime between 8 BC and AD 4 – well, that sounds like a real date.
> But does Jesus' story really start then?

(See what they say – give them a hand)

> Where did Jesus live before He came to Earth as Baby Jesus?
> **(In Heaven)**
> Why was that?

Establish that it was because He is God

> What was God doing before He came to Earth?
> Let's have a look –

Go to the beginning of the Bible

> 'In the beginning God created the Heavens and the Earth.' So God was already there, at the Beginning.[42]
> OK, now when does the story of Jesus end?

(See what they say – give them a hand if they need it)

> On the Cross?
> **(No)**
> Today, when He rises from the dead?
> **(No)**
> When He goes up to Heaven?
> **(Not even then)**
> Let's look at the Bible again – *(go to the John marker)*
> Look: the story of Jesus on Earth stops here …

Pinch together all the pages left

> but there's still all this bit of Bible to go.
> Jesus' story goes on in His Church and, let's look at the very end –

Scan the last few verses

> Yup, this is all about the End of Time.
> And it says, 'Come, Lord Jesus, Amen.'

---

42 Be careful not to suggest that God Himself has a beginning.

So Jesus is still there at the End of Time.
We're in the middle of a story.
And that's one of the reasons we've got a Paschal Candle.

THE PASCHAL CANDLE

Now this candle was lit last night/early this morning.[43]
There were no lights on in church, no candles, nothing.
And we started a bonfire outside, and lit this candle from the flames, and *Name* held it up, and we walked into church behind it, as he/she sang 'The Light of Christ!'
So this candle represents Jesus, back from the dead, getting rid of the darkness.
It's our Easter candle *(look at it intently for a moment)* and it's covered in symbols. Let's make our own candle, and see what it's about.

Pick up your candle, and in what follows see if the kids can refer to the actual candle and give you a hand with the marks and – this is the bit they like – the pins. Some Paschal Candles are difficult to read, you may have to tell them what they should be seeing

OK, this candle is Jesus, and the biggest mark on it is a …?
(Cross)
I'll mark it with a cross.

Do so, in either blue or green

Jesus died on the Cross.
Our cross is pierced by five pins.
Can anyone guess what they are?

They'll probably say 'the nails'

Almost right! They are the five wounds of Christ.
Two on His hands, Two on His feet, and the spear wound made in His side.
On the actual Paschal Candle they are little grains of incense – to remind us of the spices Jesus' body was wrapped in – encased in little wax nails. We've got little gold mapping pins.

Ask the children to help you stick them on

Now we come to an odd bit.
The Paschal Candle is so ancient, it comes from the time when

---

43 Adapt the time to local custom.

Christians spoke Greek.
And back then they wanted to say, Jesus was the Beginning and the End, the A and the Z – but they used Greek letters.
Does anyone know the Greek for 'A'?

They often do

Alpha.
Fortunately, it looks just like our A.
And what about the last letter of the Greek alphabet?
Anyone know?

Throw it open

Omega.

Use the red pen to mark the candle with the Alpha and Omega as you say

Jesus is the Alpha and the Omega,
the Beginning and the End.
And the last things we have to put on are numbers.
Can anyone see what they are?
2–0–1–8 *(or whatever year it is)*
What's that?
Yup, it's this year.
Jesus is alive right now!

Ask the children to put in the numbers. Admire the result and go through the symbols on your candle

I like the Paschal Candle, because it tells the Easter story.
The **wax** reminds us that Jesus was made of something, He was Man.
He died on the **Cross**.
But His **wounds** have turned to gold in the light of Easter Day.
He's alive *(light your candle)* and He's God.
Alpha and **Omega**, the beginning – God's always been around – and the end – and He always will be –
and, in 2018, He's with us in church this morning.

Script 22   Opening and Closing
(Easter Day Script 3)

Any of the Easter Gospels.

THEME

This session is about the wonderful hollowness of the Empty Tomb. The stone's gone, there's no one there, Jesus cannot be contained. The session uses both gesture and a 'magic' effect: have a rehearsal, work on your gestures, and try out those paper stars! (See below.) Think through the ritual of the Eucharist and work in some large movements. Some suggestions are given below – solemnly opening up the Gospel, or asking the congregation to open their hands in the *orans* position as they say the Lord's Prayer may be all you need.

SET UP

- A1 flip-chart and Pictures 22.1–22.7 and the flower template from www.canterburypress.co.uk/downloads.
- Make a traditional shop sign, with OPEN on one side and CLOSED on the other.
- Cut out flowers, see template.
- A stool with a clear bowl of water on it.
- Some cheap tiny Easter chicks.

Optional

- A bottle of champagne and somebody prepared to get the cork out of it in front of a large congregation.

ADDRESS

Start off with the shop sign – show the side that says CLOSED

> *(Ad lib)* Where do you see this?
> **(In shop windows)**

Script 22 – Opening and Closing (Easter Day Script 3)

What's written on the other side?
(OPEN)

Turn it

Yes, you're right!
Today we're going to think about things being OPEN.
At the beginning of this week, the gates of Jerusalem were open and Jesus rode through them on a donkey. And everyone who saw Him, cheered and opened their hearts to Him.
When you're feeling good, you open up. *(gesture)*

Stand up straight, open your arms wide

When you love a baby you open your arms to hold it. *(gesture)*
When you greet a friend – what do you do?

Proffer an open hand to the kids

But last week, something went wrong …
Jesus was so loving and open and fearless (*Picture 22.1*)
that some people were frightened of Him;
they got like this –

Hunch up

Judas sneaked off to betray Him. (*Picture 22.2*)
The priests got into a huddle to arrest Him. (*Picture 22.3*)
Even Jesus' disciples curled up and went to sleep. (*Picture 22.4*)
And suddenly all those welcoming hands that Jesus saw on Palm Sunday …

Wave

Turned into this –

Clench fist

Now when you are in this sort of mood –

Hunch up again

You start doing horrible things
You close things: you close doors, you close your heart.
You want to get people as small as you, scrunch them up, lock them up, get rid of them …
you don't want free happy people upsetting you.
So Jesus was beaten, and killed and locked up in a tomb (*Picture 22.5a*)

Script 22 – Opening and Closing (Easter Day Script 3)

> And they put a great big heavy stone on it. (*Picture 22.5b*)
> Clonk!
> And they thought, 'That's it, we've got Him boxed up – no more Jesus!'
> But life isn't like that.
> You can't really get rid of free natural things.
> You can't stop a spring of water – if you do, it'll turn up somewhere else –
> do you know, you can't even get rid of a little paper flower.
> Watch this, I'm going to pretend that I hate this flower.
> I'm going to scrunch it and fold it and make it small. Hah!

Make a tight little packet of the flower with all its petals tucked in – the flowers template – have some other stars to hand, already folded

> Ugh! And here's some horrid clean water, I'll throw all these rubbishy stars in that –

Produce the clear glass bowl of water and throw the packets on the surface; they unfold rather miraculously – and if you've coloured their insides with a water soluble yellow pen, they turn the water gold

> Isn't that amazing – the star has come back as a crown.
> Well, if that happens to a paper star – what do you think happens to the Son of God?
> Even as He died Jesus spread His arms wide and open on the cross.

Refer to any large crucifix nearby

> You can pile all this stuff on Him, and shove Him in a cave,
> and put a stone across the door,
> but you can't stop Jesus (*Picture 22.6*) opening it up –
> rising from the Tomb.
> That's what today is about.
> Every Christian stands taller today – let's see you do it.

Stand tall

> And they open their hands to receive gifts
> Let's see some open hands –

Hand out some of the little chicks

> Do you know why we like chicks so much at Easter?
> Because they break out of their egg shells.

OPTIONAL EXTRA

>Do you know why it's a pious act to drink champagne today? *(rhetorical question)*
>Because the cork pops out of the bottle.

Demo from server and champagne bottle – be sensible where you point the bottle, make sure the cork goes up in the air and nowhere near the kids

>And the bubbles whizz up to the top
>And because it's right and proper to feast on Easter Day.

BACK TO THE SCRIPT

>Look at the things we're surrounded by today – chicks, flowers, eggs, champagne corks. Loads of things breaking out, popping off and springing into life. Just like Jesus, springing out of the grave.

Address this bit to the adults – the church will doubtless be full of visitors and stray Christians

>And He didn't go back. Jesus went straight to His friends, huddled together behind a closed door, and He flung that door open.
>And He comes to us, too – to our closed hearts, to that bit of us that won't let go and believe He's opened the doors of life.
>'Open up!' is one of the great Easter cries.

Link this with whatever open gesture you've decided to emphasize in the Mass

>We've opened the Gospels in the midst of the people, we are going to open our arms in prayer.

Show the congregation the orans gesture for the Our Father

>We will open our arms to greet each other at the Peace,
>open our hands to receive Jesus at Communion, and we'll be sent out through the open doors of the church at the end of the service, to wish everyone a Happy Easter and spread the Good News.

Add in whatever Easter custom you finish the Eucharist with

>Once we've opened a spot of champagne and rolled a few eggs – *after* Holy Communion …

Script 23   Rock and Roll

(Easter Day Script 4)

John 20.1–9

> **THEME**
>
> This is such an elaborate homily to set up that I've tucked it in as a makeweight. Kids love it as it's mildly anarchic …

SET UP

- A Hot Cross Bun.
- A small framed tent in a dull colour – to look like the Tomb.
- A hula hoop covered in grey paper or fabric, to represent the stone. You should still be able to roll it.
- A folded sheet and napkin inside the tent.
- Some servers to bring it on, with a minimum of fuss.
- Three children prepared to run up and down the main aisle as Mary, Peter and John.
- Some *very* hard boiled eggs, coloured if you've got the time. Boiling them wrapped in onion skin gives them a pleasant arty look, or just use food dye.

ADDRESS

Happy Easter, everyone!
What's the best bit about Easter?
(**Eggs!**)
I thought you'd say that.
Actually there's a lot of special food around at this time of year.
Like this …

Hold up the Hot Cross Bun. Establish what it is, and why it's got a cross on it.

Script 23 – Rock and Roll (Easter Day Script 4)

Yes, Jesus died on the Cross. When was that?
(On Good Friday)
That was last Friday. And Jesus' friends took down His Body and buried Him in a tomb. It was a cave in a rock, and looked a bit like this …

Some servers set up the Tomb; ask them to tuck the grave clothes inside without the kids noticing

Then they rolled a stone over the opening.

Roll the covered hoop over the opening

And that was that.
Until this morning, Sunday, when Mary Magdalene went to the Tomb, and came running back with some incredible news. What was it?

See if the kids can remember the Easter Gospel. Get them to be quite precise. Names? Who came first? Did they see Jesus? What did they see? Remember it together

It's an odd story, isn't it? Let's run it …

Choose a Mary Magdalene, a Peter and a John; send them down to the end of the church

So, Mary gets to the Tomb first …

Mary runs up

What does she actually see?
(The Tomb is open, the stone has been rolled away)
What, like this?

Roll the rock away

OK, then Mary runs back to Peter and John …

Off she goes

Have you got there yet?
Right, she tells Peter and John – and they run down.

John gets here first, so make sure he leads

OK, chaps, run!

They run up

Right, now John sees the Tomb, but doesn't go inside – he kneels here.
But Peter peers inside – anything in there, Peter?

Script 23 – Rock and Roll (Easter Day Script 4)

Encourage Peter to pull out the folded-up sheet

> That's what they wrapped Jesus' Body in – shake it out.

Peter and John do so

> Hmm, no Jesus … Is He in the Tomb?
> (**No**)
> Well, where is He?
> And, guys, who moved the rock?

Roll the stone back

> Mary! Can you come back here again?

Mary runs up

	Did you move the rock?
Mary	No!
Preacher	Did you chaps move it?
Peter and John	No!
Preacher	Anyone here heard of rock and roll? What is it?
	(**Pop music/whatever**)
	Well, this rock rolled –

Roll it off again

> Anyone heard of the Rolling Stones? *(don't wait for an answer)*
> Somebody roll that back to me *(catch it)* because this is the most amazing Rolling Stone I've ever heard of.
> The stone in front of Jesus' Tomb weighed tons, yet it rolled away. Who rolled it?

See what they say – some kids will tell you it was the angel, or perhaps it was Jesus. Somebody usually says 'God rolled it'

Ad lib into

> Lots of people have tried to guess, but I think *Name* is right, God rolled it.
> Why was that?

(Kids usually say 'to let Jesus out')

> Yup, OK. But do you think Jesus needed the stone to be moved? Once He was risen He could walk through doors!

See what they say, establish that the stone was probably moved so the disciples would understand that Jesus wasn't there

That was the first big surprise on Easter morning – a large empty cave, and a rolling stone.

To the adults

Well, the disciples still had to find Jesus that first Easter morning; it wasn't very difficult because He wanted to be found,
and we have to find Him too.
He's still alive, here in this church –
and we can find Him – in our hearts, in His friends, and at the altar.
But sometimes it feels as if we've got a big stone inside us, blocking up the entrance.
God can move that stone; ask Him to roll it away – because Jesus' life and joy is just waiting to burst through.

Back to the kids

Now what I really wanted to do this morning was roll a great big boulder down the aisle, to show you how exciting it is when a stone really gets moving. But you can see what's behind me – nothing but grown-ups and, you know what? They didn't fancy it –

Mock dismay, get the other clergy to respond with a panto 'Ah!'

However, we have got *(produce hard boiled eggs)* these!
Specially prepared Easter eggs, boiled nice and hard, so we can roll them at the end of Mass.
So, every time you eat an egg today, remember that first Easter morning: you can roll eggs, God can roll stones – and Jesus Christ is out of His Tomb, risen from the dead.

ROLLING EGGS

The best time to roll eggs is after the Post-Communion prayer and before the Blessing. Get some fall guys – like the church wardens – at the end of the main aisle and bowl a couple of eggs down to them. The kids will almost certainly cluster round to help. If you bless chocolate eggs in your church, the small filled ones are just as good for rolling as real eggs – anything hollow, however, is useless.

Script 24   Eastertide
(The Walk to Emmaus)

Luke 24.13–35

> **THEME**
>
> The walk and supper at Emmaus is such a rich Gospel that it's difficult to know what to home in on. This session concentrates on the way the narrative parallels the sequence of the Liturgy of the Word and Eucharist at Mass.

SET UP

- Narrator.
- Someone to play Jesus: in this instance it helps if it's a man or a large teenager.
- Alb for Jesus, plus large clerical cloak and a hat (as like the one worn by Indiana Jones in *The Raiders of the Lost Ark* as possible …).
- Small pocket Bible for Jesus.
- Small draped table, two stools, pitta bread on a plate.
- Extra priest's wafer set on the altar.
- Run through the script with your 'Jesus' beforehand.

Gather the children down the front; Jesus in an alb sits by the side

ADDRESS

Ad lib on the fact it's still Easter

> We're in white/gold, the Paschal Candle is still burning, and we're so happy that Jesus has come back from the dead that we keep saying 'Alleluia'.
> The thing about Easter is that it's not only happy, it's full of surprising new ideas. You see, Jesus knew He was due to go back to Heaven, so He had to get His friends used to the idea that, though He'd still be around, He'd be around in a different way.

WALKING WITH JESUS

> So He put on a big cloak ...

Jesus stands up and envelops himself in a cloak

Puts on hat

> and a large hat, and went for a walk.
> Two of His friends were ahead of Him on the road – feeling really fed up. They didn't know that Jesus was back from the dead, and they had their heads down, and their arms folded.
> Can anyone do that?

Choose a couple of volunteers, and set them walking down a side aisle. (Take a view on the size of your church, they need to make a small circuit and get back to the middle)

> Yep, good. Well, it didn't take long for Jesus to catch them up, and He started walking with them.

LISTENING TO JESUS

> And as they walked, Jesus pulled out a Bible and began to talk –

Jesus pulls out a Bible and mimes earnest talk

> Jesus' friends didn't realize who He was, but they loved hearing Him talk. They even stopped for a moment and looked in His Bible.

They do so

> Anyway, they went on walking.

Cue walking

> And Jesus' friends began to cheer up. They felt their hearts get lighter, and a strange warmth in their chest ...

KNOWING JESUS IS CLOSE

To everyone

> Put your hands on your hearts, shut your eyes for a minute.

Do so yourself. Pause

> Can you feel your hand next to your chest? That's how close Jesus felt to them.

EATING WITH JESUS

Jesus and the kids should be back at the front by now

> So, when they got to their house, Jesus' friends asked the stranger in for supper.

Gesture from kids – they gather round the set table, kids sit on each side, Jesus sits between them and, taking his cue from you, he takes, blesses and breaks the bread

> They sat at table and Jesus picked up the bread,
> Blessed it,
> Broke it,
> And gave it to them.
> And suddenly they realized who He was! They jumped to their feet

The kids jump up

> And at that very moment, Jesus disappeared.

Jesus ducks behind the table and is hidden by the tablecloth. He quietly removes his hat and cloak

TELLING PEOPLE ABOUT JESUS

> The friends looked at each other, then down at the broken bread – 'That was Jesus!' they said.
> And they rushed back to Jerusalem to tell Jesus' other friends what they had seen.

The two kids move swiftly back to sit with the other children

> Well, Jesus doesn't come to Earth in His earthly body any more, but He's still around.

Jesus stands up in his alb

> He still **walks** with His friends – He walked with us to church this morning. He's with us right now.

Jesus sits in a front pew with some adults. Make sure he's ultra-gentle and polite – 'Do you mind if I sit here?'

> He was in the Bible as we heard in the Readings.

Jesus goes across to the lectern

> He **spoke** to us in the Gospel.

He holds up the Gospel book

> He's **beside** us as we pray – right near our hearts.

Jesus sits with the children

        And He will be with us when we **break bread** together.

Jesus moves to the altar, holds up the priest's wafer, breaks it – and exits

        We can't see His hands and feet – but we can touch and eat the Bread, it has become His Body.

        Jesus is alive, that's why – at the end of Mass – the priest tells us to be like Jesus' mates and **tell** everyone about Him.

        OK, we're going on with the rest of the Eucharist now, ready to greet Jesus when He joins us at the Breaking of the Bread.

Script 25   Ascension Day

Acts 1 and Luke 24

> **THEME**
>
> Ascension is an excellent feast to celebrate with children, whether you have a special service on the day itself (fortieth day after Easter, a Thursday) or, with the Roman Catholics, designate Easter 7 as Ascension Sunday. The story comes with slightly bizarre pictures, and the narrative is so interesting that it often provokes useful questions such as 'Where is Heaven?', 'Why did Jesus go?' and 'Did He really go up?'

SET UP

- A1 flip-chart and marker pen.
- Blu Tack or some such adhesive.
- Pictures 25.1–25.10 from www.canterburypress.co.uk/downloads.
- Look round your church. Are there steps up to your sanctuary? Have you got a raised pulpit nearby? You need another level. In extremis, bring in a step ladder.
- With any luck, your easel is on a platform; if it isn't, create a shallow step next to it using whatever is to hand – a box, a kid's chair, a little dais …
- This is a very good service at which to use incense.

ADDRESS

JESUS' ASCENSION

Today we come to the end of Jesus' earthly life. It was time for Him to go home and take His place beside His Heavenly Father. Let's remember the story together.

You and the children tell the story again, using the accounts you have just heard in the Reading and the Gospel (Acts 1 and Luke 24), and sticking up Pictures 25.1–25.8. They include a hill, the disciples plus, Our Lady, Jesus blessing and ascending, the cloud (which covers the Jesus figure completely) and two angels

It's a good story, isn't it? Let's reel back –

Take off the cloud, Jesus, and the angels

>OK, now suppose you and I had gone up the hill with Jesus' friends *(add Picture 25.9 of a couple of kids)*, what do you think we would have seen?
>We'd have seen Jesus, blessing us *(put Jesus on the hill)* – and then what?
>We know He went up – that's why the angels say, 'Hey, guys, why are you looking *up?*'
>But did He whoosh up to Heaven like a sky rocket?

Zoom Jesus up the chart and off into space

>No, because to start with Heaven isn't in space, and anyway Jesus hadn't gone very far before a cloud covered Him.
>Some artists when they draw this think the cloud covered Jesus so quickly that all His friends saw was His feet

Put cloud back, making sure Jesus' feet show

>It looks a bit odd, doesn't it?
>Some people think that Jesus went so quickly ...

Cover the feet with the cloud

>that He disappeared, and the disciples started looking round to see where He'd gone *(add Picture 25.10 of the disciples)*, and saw His footprints in the grass.

Draw in Jesus' footprints on the hill

>'Look! He was here a minute ago ...'
>I think Jesus went quietly up, a little way, and simply disappeared.

ASCENDING

>Let's try some ascending. Which way do you go when you ascend – just point –

(The kids will point up)

>OK, how far can we ascend in this bit of the church?

Go with the flow – send a sensible kid to mount the sanctuary steps, or go into the pulpit, or – if the organist agrees – into the organ loft. If it's all flat look round and say –

>Hey, what about that step ladder?

Hold it firm and let a kid go up

So *Name* has ascended – it was pretty good, wasn't it?
But you don't actually have to go up very far to ascend.

Ask another kid forward

Watch this …
OK, *Name*, go up this step.

The child goes up one step

Yup, she's ascended.
But supposing she not only ascends but goes slightly sideways?

Cue the child to do it again, but this time disappear behind the easel

Ah! Now she's ascended and disappeared.
That's what Jesus did.
Let's think about that

Change of mood – it might be an idea to sit with the kids

Where did Jesus go when He ascended?
(Heaven)
Yep, home to Heaven. Now the point is, where is Heaven?
(The sky/space/above us/we don't know – *take what comes*)

HEAVEN

OK, well there's a couple of things we do know about Heaven.
It's not a place – not like London – you can't get there by aeroplane, you won't find it behind a cloud, or even in outer space.
Heaven is where God is. And Jesus went back to God.
Well, guys, how far away *is* God?

(See what they say, but establish how quickly God hears our prayers, how happy He is to be near us, in our hearts, in our troubles, at the altar)

God is very near – close but hidden.
He's like our thoughts.
Can you see them?
(Nope)
Where are they? *(rhetorical)*
Hidden in our heads.
Or like our hearts.
Let's feel our hearts for a moment.

Press your hand on your chest

> I can feel my hand on my heart.
> I can feel my heart beating.
> It's close, but hidden.
> And that's what Heaven is like, very close to us, but hidden.
> That's where Jesus is –

Back to the easel

> We've been thinking what *we* would have seen if we'd stood on the hill with Jesus' disciples.
> Let's think what Jesus saw as He ascended.
> For a moment He saw His friends' faces looking up

Add picture, or draw faces via the template

> but very quickly He saw His disciples like this …

Add or draw a couple of profiles

> That's what people look like when you're sitting near them.
> Once Jesus was in Heaven, He could be close to them again.
>
> You see, once Jesus had ascended, He didn't have to walk round the Earth, going from Jerusalem to Jericho – just think how long it would have taken Him to get to *St (name of your church)* – to see His friends, He could be everywhere.
> Heaven is everywhere because God is everywhere.

OPTIONAL EXTRA

Ask a server to bring the thurible over

> It's like this incense.

Load thurible

> Watch the smoke as it rises, and spreads out, and fills the church. It's one of the reasons we use incense, it reminds us that God is everywhere.

BACK TO SCRIPT

> Jesus is here this morning, sitting beside us in the pews, filling our church like the incense, present in the Bread and the Wine.
> Let's remember how close He is to us when we come to kneel before Him at the altar.

Script 26   Pentecost

Acts 2.1–11 and John 20.19–23

THEME

A session on air or, rather, on the mighty rushing wind that attended the descent of the Holy Spirit on the Apostles at Pentecost.[44]

SET UP

- A large air-filled ball, like a netball or a football (if you happen to have a soggy ball, bring that along too).
- Cushion.
- Snorkel or a picture of a diver, or a toy astronaut (make sure his visor is down).
- Several uninflated balloons. Blow them up and let the air out beforehand, so they blow up easily in performance.
- An empty thurible (or foil barbecue tray), charcoal, matches.
- A1 flip-chart plus black and red marker pens.
- Hand-held fan.
- Plastic straw and a ping pong ball.
- Have the text of the Post Communion prayer (below) ready for the priest if it's one you don't use often.

GOSPEL

This homily uses the account of the first Pentecost in the Reading, Acts 2.1–11, and the Gospel, John 20.19–23

---

[44] There is a session on the mysterious properties of fire in *Creative Ideas for Children's Worship: Year C*, Script 48, 'Fire!' This can be adapted to a Pentecost sermon if you run the candle and charcoal demos to illustrate the way the Holy Spirit enflamed the Early Church with the burning love of God.

ADDRESS

Start off with the ball

>OK, I want you to watch this

Start bouncing it

>Can any of you do that? *(with any luck you'll get a star performer)* What's making it bounce?

(You might get 'you are' or 'the floor', establish it's the air inside the ball.

Write AIR up on the flip-chart. If you happen to have a soggy ball, pull it out – 'look at this, it's useless', otherwise, try and bounce the cushion – hopeless

>Air makes things bounce.

Write BOUNCE on the flip-chart

>Watch this –

Blow up one of the uninflated balloons and let it go. This usually goes down well – let off a couple more

>Air makes things move.

Write MOVE on the flip-chart

>Let's think about some other things air does

Pull out your snorkel, or pictures of divers/astronauts/anyone with breathing apparatus.

Talk them through – why do they need this stuff in water or in space?

>Because there's no air.
>Air makes things live.

Write LIVE on the flip-chart

>And one last thing …

Ask the thurifer to bring over the empty thurible. Cluster the children round, pull out some charcoal, and light it, describing what you are doing – 'Can anyone see the little sparks as the charcoal catches?'

>Now *Name* is going to swing the thurible – that's to get air moving round the charcoal. We want it to burn, and it can't burn without air.

Move the children back as the thurifer swings the censer. Watch the charcoal and see if the kids can spot the moment when it goes red. Blow on it, it will glow redder

>Air makes things burn, it **enflames** them …

Write ENFLAME on the flip-chart (in red)

> OK, I think we're up to speed on air, but there's one really odd thing about it. We can't see it …
> It's really important, and totally invisible.
> How do we know it exists?

(See what they come up with)

Pull out the fan and start fanning the air

> I'm moving the air about, can you see it?
> **(No)**
> Ask the kids to shut their eyes

Fan their faces but, because small children don't like this very much, choose a brave ten-year-old

> Can you feel it?
> We can feel air – and we can see what it does. Look …

Blow through a straw to move a ping pong ball across the floor – or get an agile server to do it for you

> What's moving the ball?
> **(Air)**
> How do you know? *(Children are usually very good at explaining you can know things by their effects.)*
> OK, I get it, we can't see it, but we can see what it does.
> I think that's why the Holy Spirit came as air.
> You see, the Holy Spirit is God – can you see God?
> **(No)**

Incarnation

Don't use this unless a child reminds you of Jesus or indeed the Host.

God *could* be seen when He came to Earth as a man – Jesus. And we see Him when He becomes present in the Bread at Mass. But God Himself does not have a body.

Script 26 – Pentecost

BACK TO THE SCRIPT

> Why's that? *(rhetorical)*
> Because God is spirit.
> Spirit is something we can't see, that hasn't got a body.
> Well, spirit might be invisible – but it's real!
> The Apostles knew at once that something amazing was happening on the first Pentecost.
> The Holy Spirit rushed into their room like a mighty wind, blowing their hair about, and setting little tongues of fire flickering above their heads.
> And though the Holy Spirit isn't made of air – He certainly knew how to use it.

Circle the words MOVE, LIVE, ENFLAME etc. as you talk about the effects of the Spirit

> He **blew** those apostles out of the room, and they ran out to tell people about Jesus. They felt **alive**, and they felt the love of God, like a **flame** warming their hearts as they started their new job.
> Did you catch what their new job was?
> **(To tell people about Jesus)**
> Yup, and it's our job too.
> The Holy Spirit has never left the Church.
> Listen out for Him in the rest of the service.
> There's a great moment at the end of Mass when we ask God to 'Send us out, in the power of the Spirit,
> to live and work to your praise and glory.'
> And I'm sure if the priest could blow us out of the doors at the end of the service, he/she would!

POST-COMMUNION PRAYER AT THE END OF THE SERVICE

> Almighty God,
> we thank you for feeding us
> with the Body and Blood of your Son Jesus Christ.
> Through Him we offer You our souls and bodies
> to be a living sacrifice.
> Send us out in the power of your Spirit
> to live and work to your praise and glory. **Amen**

Script 27 Trinity Sunday

Matthew 28.16–20 or John 3.5–7, 16

> **THEME**
>
> How do you explain the Holy Trinity? You can't. One day we may just *see* how God can be Three Persons and One God, but in this life the Holy Trinity is something to be experienced and adored, but not explained.[45] This session introduces the kids to some beings even more limited than us, to encourage us in the hope that one day we will understand God a little better.

SET UP

- A1 flip-chart and marker pen. The pictures for this are so easy that anyone can draw them, see the template of the Holy Trinity from www.canterburypress.co.uk/downloads.
- One shape, the Perfect Square, complete with beatific smile, should be pre-drawn and cut out, so it can be flown on and off the flip-chart.
- The first page of the flip-chart should be blank. The second page should have some shapes drawn on it, with no expressions, and enough room for the Perfect Square to be stuck in their midst.
- A large cardboard cube, covered in white paper, and marked up as per the template. Have the box to hand, but hidden from the kids.

ADDRESS

Start off by talking about 3D TV

> What's the difference between 3D cinema and ordinary cinema?

Establish that things look solid on 3D TV and talk through the three dimensions

> On ordinary TV things look flat, like the shape I'm drawing on this flip-chart.

---

[45] I am convinced that the nun I overheard once, talking briskly to a group of kids on the subject, got it absolutely right, 'The Holy Trinity? Ah, now, that's a holy mystery ...'

Draw a rectangle
> They've got height and width but they haven't got depth.

Indicate depth with your hands. Don't use or refer to any 3D object or you'll spoil the punch line below
> Imagine what it would be like to live in 2D …

Draw a face in the rectangle (see template throughout for expressions)
> You'd be called a 'flatlander'.

Run your hands down the paper to emphasise its flatness
> Well, I'm going to tell you a story about some Flatlanders.

Draw the shapes as you speak
> They came in all sorts of shapes, and some were good and some were bad,
> and some were cheerful – and others were not. *(draw in their expressions)*
> In fact, they were very like us.
> And one day a wonderful shape appeared among them.

Turn the page and stick on the Perfect Square
> All the Flatlanders thought he was wonderful.

Draw in a few cheery expressions near the Perfect Square
> And the Perfect Square told the Flatlanders about a wonderful shape who lived in Heaven and who loved them all.
> 'What sort of shape is He?' they asked.
> 'Well, He's a sort of square,' said the Perfect Square.
> 'So He looks like you?'
> 'No,' said the Square, 'He's like six squares, but there's only one of Him.'
> 'What?' said the Flatlanders.
> 'Don't worry about it, when you get to Heaven, you'll see.'

Put in a couple of wary eyes on one of the shapes (see template)
> And with that he twinkled away

Fly the Perfect Square out
> Well, the shapes tried to remember what he'd told them.
> And they had a go at loving the great shape in Heaven,
> and they said prayers to the One and the Six, and sometimes they imagined the Heavenly Square as six squares, and sometimes as one enormous square …

Draw in puzzled faces and thought bubbles with '6' in one and '1' in another

> And the shapes who were good at theology came up with brilliant creeds and formulas, and the ones who weren't theological got muddled – and lots of shapes just loved the Heavenly Square and said it was a holy mystery.
> BUT when they died and went to Heaven, they left Flatland behind and entered another world – and there they *saw* the wonderful being the Perfect Square had told them about.

Hold up the cube

> And they realized immediately how something could be 6 and 1.
> *(turn the cube)*
> They didn't need any explanations.
> What had happened?
> **(They'd got into a three-dimensional world)**
> Exactly!
> Well, we don't worship cubes or shapes or even Perfect Squares.
> We worship God.

Turn the page and write 'God' in the centre

> How many Gods are there?

(One – put any child anxious to tell you about the Persons of the Trinity on hold for a moment)

> And when we pray to God, we call Him three things.

Go through the Sign of the Cross with them

> We say, '✠ In the Name of the Father and of the Son and of the Holy Spirit.'
> How many is that?
> **(Three)**

Write up 'Father', 'Son' and 'Holy Spirit' round the word 'God'

> Are there three Gods then?
> **(Establish there is just one God)**
> There is one God, and we know Him as Three Persons.
> God is One and Three.
> He is called the Holy Trinity.
> We can't explain the Trinity, but that's OK.
> We pray to God the Father, we listen to God the Son, and we feel God the Spirit in our hearts.
> And we worship the one true God.

Script 27 – Trinity Sunday   111

We don't have to understand Him – I don't understand how my iPhone works, but I can still switch it on.
And anyway, when we get to Heaven we shall see God – and it will be quite obvious how He can be One and Three.
But I can tell you one thing – He won't turn out to be a geometrical shape.

Toss away the cube

He'll be something *much* more wonderful …

Script 28   Bread from Heaven
(Corpus Christi)

St John 6.51–58

This homily can be used for:

- Corpus Christi (The Gospel is from Year A).
- Teaching children about the Eucharist.
- Any Family Mass in which the Gospel is taken from John 6. (There's a run of them in Year B, Propers 11–15.)

This session assumes that a bell is rung as the priest elevates the Host during the Prayer of Consecration.

THEME

'I am the Bread of Life.' This was one of Jesus' most complex sayings, couched in the simplest of words. It's because He *is* the Bread of Life that we gather at the Eucharist every week. This is a great opportunity to introduce the children to the central action of the service, the taking and blessing of bread. Fortunately, with a fresh loaf to hand, you'll get the children's attention immediately. This session uses the story of the desert monks, St Paul and St Antony, to show how even saints look up when food is mentioned.

SET UP

- A1 flip-chart and some marker pens.
- The template of grain etc. and Pictures 28.1–28.6 from www.canterburypress.co.uk/downloads.
- A fresh loaf of bread.
- A communion wafer.
- A ciborium.
- A server ready to demonstrate the ringing of the bell at the Elevation.

Script 28 – Bread from Heaven (Corpus Christi)

GOSPEL   St John 6.51–58 plus verses 60

Read the Gospel in the way you would at any Eucharist. Preface the reading with the words 'Jesus said …'

You may prefer to shorten the Gospel by cutting out verses 54–57

ADDRESS

A DIFFICULT GOSPEL

> It's a tough Gospel today. Jesus tells His friends that He is the Bread from Heaven and they don't understand Him.
> Did you hear what they said? 'This teaching is too hard – who can listen to it?'
> Well, if Jesus' friends didn't understand Him, I don't know what we're going to do at *St (name of your church)*, but let's have a go.
> What shall we start with?
> I know, bread! *(hold up a nice fresh loaf)*

FOOD

> It looks nice, doesn't it?
> There's something about food – you can't help looking up when it's mentioned.
> God knows that, and He knows how much we need it. So He feeds us.
> Though actually He doesn't normally give us bread ready made like this. He likes us to do a bit of work too.

Over to the flip-chart

> So God gives us
> **grain, earth, rain** and **sun.**

Draw these from the template; ask the children to help you. They're good at rain

> And we put it all together and we get **bread**
> But sometimes God does a fast forward.
> Let me tell you the story of St Paul and St Anthony.

ST PAUL AND ST ANTONY

We'll start with St Paul.
There are lots of saints called Paul. This one lived in the third century AD – and he was a rich young Roman (*Pictures 28.1 & 28.2*)
But one day he decided to give up all his super clothes,
his sun specs and fast chariots and become a hermit. (*Picture 28.3*)
He wanted to live alone in the desert and be very close to God.
Not many people are called to be hermits, and I think God takes special care of the people who are. Most hermits are very sensible, but Paul could only think about God, so he found a really lonely place, with a stream running by – and he completely forgot to work out how he was going to eat.
So every day God sent him a raven – with a loaf of bread. (*Picture 28.4*)

Do a zoom noise as you bring the raven in at the top of the picture

And every time Paul heard the raven, he looked up. And that's how he lived for years and years until, one day, another hermit – St Anthony – dropped in for a visit. (*Picture 28.5 and remove Picture 28.4*)
The two saints had lots to talk about and they talked and prayed together all day and, just as St Anthony was wondering where supper was, they heard the sound of the raven.

Slightly flap your elbows as you say creak! creak! creak!

Rather slower today …
Both the saints looked up, and in he came, (*Picture 28.6*)
and sat on a rock wiping his brow with his wing.
He'd brought *two* loaves of bread.

Ad lib, this is a throwaway

God knew that St Paul would be needing double rations.
That sort of thing doesn't happen very often.

FOOD FOR BODY AND SOUL

God knows we've got bodies, and that our bodies need food, so He provides us with food.
But we're not just bodies – we've got souls as well – the life inside us that makes us want to pray, to love people, and please God.
That needs feeding too, and God feeds our souls with Himself.

And He gives Himself to us in the Bread of the Eucharist.

Hold up some unconsecrated bread

It's quite different, isn't it?
Really small.
We need this sort of bread *(hold up the loaf)* when we need fuel to get our bodies going.
But our souls aren't like that. They need food too – but their food is God Himself, and He can fit Himself into anything – He can become Baby Jesus, or fit into a human heart or into a tiny piece of bread.

THE BREAD OF HEAVEN

So this is the bread we'll be using this Mass. It hasn't been blessed yet, but we'll put it in the ciborium

Ask a child to place it in the ciborium

and, when the priest says the great prayer at the altar, he/she will ask God to come and fill the bread with Himself.
It'll go on looking like ordinary bread, but it will also be God.
Once a piece of bread is blessed it's called the Host.
Watch carefully when the priest goes to the altar today.
The priest will take the bread, and bless it – then hold it up.
Sometimes we pray by speaking and sometimes by doing something.
Holding up the bread is a prayer.
And God always answers, and becomes present in the Bread.
You can't miss this moment as the server will ring a bell. Like this …

Ask the server to ding the bell three times

The moment you hear that bell, look up – the Host has become the Bread of Heaven.
That's what Jesus meant, all those years ago, when He said He was the Bread that came from Heaven. He was and will always be food to us.
His friends didn't understand Him because the Church and the Mass hadn't happened yet. But *we* know what He meant – that's why we're here.

So let's put this ciborium on the *(whatever the customary place is for the ciborium in your church)* and get ready for the most holy part of Mass: the Breaking of the Bread.

Script 29 The Feasts of Saints Peter and Paul

(29 June)

Matthew 16.13–19

> **THEME**
>
> It's good to know that, given their chequered friendship on Earth, Saints Peter and Paul share a feast day in Heaven. People are usually ordained at this time,[46] and this session introduces the kids to any new deacon or priest who is joining the clergy team. Even if you aren't welcoming a new curate, it's not a bad moment to reflect on the ordained ministry and what clerics wear – and why. Two sessions are offered below, one for a deacon, another for a new priest. In both cases you need to ask the newcomer if they'd be prepared to join in the sermon dressed in their cassock, and put on their liturgical clothes (on cue) from the amice upwards. They also assume the use of traditional garments (alb, amice, rope girdle, stole, dalmatic or chasuble). The sessions work with a cassock alb, but the other forms of Anglican gear (simple clerical collar, suit, jeans) aren't covered.

SET UP FOR DEACON

- Any bit of clothing or headgear that is job-specific – a Fireman Sam helmet, policeman's helmet, crown – anything obvious.
- A1 flip-chart, Pictures 29.1–29.10 and cutting instructions from www.canterburypress.co.uk/downloads.
- Lavabo (bowl), jug and napkin. Ask some servers to be on hand to show how it's done.
- The deacon's garments in a neat pile, stacked in the order he/she will put them on.

---

46 Its traditional title is 'Petertide'. St Paul often doesn't get much of a look-in.

- Ask the deacon to practise knotting his/her rope girdle.
- A large waiter's apron, a white sheet will do, plus a dish or glass to polish.

SET UP FOR PRIEST

- A1 flip-chart.
- A yoke – a real one if you've got one, but a wooden broom handle or similar will do just as well.
- Two heavy-looking bundles (stuffed with paper). They should be secured by a loop, so they can be attached to the ends of the yoke.
- The priest's garments in a neat pile, stacked in the order he/she will put them on.
- Talk through the final dialogue with the new priest beforehand.

ADDRESS

INTRODUCING A NEW DEACON

Ad lib about Petertide, it being the time of year when people are ordained as priests or deacons

> And we're very lucky at *St (name of your church)* to be having *(Mother/Father N)*, who was ordained last *(whenever)* and is joining us as a deacon.
> Let's think about deacons. What do they do?
> Well, we can often tell what people do by the clothes they wear.
> Who wears this?

Show them your helmet, crown, whatever …

> **(Correct answer guaranteed)**
> Exactly!

WAITER

Introduce the children to the waiter and the use of a large apron

> Watch as *(he/she)* puts it on …
> It's huge, isn't it?
> Who wears this sort of thing?
> **(A waiter)**
> Why's it so big?

See what the kids think; the waiter helps by wiping his/her hands, polishing a plate – first spitting on it (always goes down well)

Yes, the apron is like a towel.
So, a waiter or a fireman has the right sort of clothes for their job. And so does a deacon, except, as their costume is hundreds of years old, we don't always notice this.
Let's go back to the fourth century ...

Put up Pictures 29.1 and 29.2 of a fourth-century Roman gent (in underpants) and slave (ditto) with clothes the kids can stick on

Here are two fourth-century chaps.
They look very alike, don't they? Actually, they're not – but we can only spot the difference when we dress them ...

Put the cut-out clothes on Picture 29.1, and comment on his long white tunic (Picture 29.3), sandals (Picture 29.4) (they had to be tied) belt (Picture 29.5) (also tied), scarf (Picture 29.6) if it's cold (also tied), topped off by a cloak (Picture 29.7).

The cloak was called a toga – until some cool dudes from a place called Dalmatia came up with a new version of the cloak ...

Put on the long-sleeved version of the cloak (Picture 29.8)

They called it a dalmatic.
Well, whatever cloak he was wearing, anyone seeing this chap would know he was a gent. Loads of clothes, nice colours, and look how *long* everything is. You can only wear long clothes if you don't have to do heavy work. This chap could write, or rule a country, but he couldn't dig roads.
Now this guy ...

Turn to the slave in Picture 29.2

worked all the time. He's a slave. And he wears ...

Add the simple short-skirted, short-sleeved tunic (Picture 29.9)

Why do you suppose it's so short?
Yup, he's got a lot of work to do.
Sometimes he added things ...
An apron perhaps
or a towel.
Slaves were always on hand with jugs and bowls of water and towels so their master and his guests could wash off the dust of Rome.
They'd offer them a jug and a bowl, just as we do in Mass.

Script 29 – The Feasts of Saints Peter and Paul (29 June)

Bring some acolytes forward (kids if possible) with the water bowl etc. for the lavabo; ask them to demonstrate

> At Mass the priest just washes his fingers, but Romans washed their hands and feet, so they needed bigger towels, and slaves often slung the towels over their shoulders, tied in a knot at the waist – like this – so they had a good handful of towel ready.

Add diagonal towel to the slave (Picture 29.10)

> And, if you looked at this chap you'd think, immediately, *slave!*
> Well, this is the fourth century. The Romans weren't politically correct and slaves were at the bottom of the pile. And they knew it. Nobody wanted to be a slave.
> Servants looked like this too, they were at least paid – but nobody thought much of them either. What you wanted to be was a gent!
> OK, now we need to get our heads round a couple of Greek words.

Write up 'doulos' for slave and 'diakonos' for servant. (Many people in the Roman Empire spoke Greek as their first language)

> The fourth century was a good time for Christians. We weren't persecuted any more and we began to build churches and fill them with beautiful things. And we wanted our priests and ministers to look super too, so they were dressed as Roman gentlemen. They still are – watch.

Enter the curate, in cassock, and gets robed; give him/her a hand and ad lib on the amount of help he/she needs

> That's one of the features of being a gent, you have people to help you get dressed.
> First a scarf to keep the draughts out – the amice.
> Then a long white tunic – the alb.
> And a girdle, which has to be knotted.
> Everything is tied, you notice – the Romans never got round to inventing buttons.
> And then it's all topped off with a poncho toga, or a long-sleeved one. *(chasuble and dalmatic)*
> Well, the chasuble is worn by a priest and a dalmatic is worn by a deacon. Which are you *(Mother/Father)*?

New deacon   A deacon!
Preacher   OK, so *Mother/Father N* is going for the fashionable dalmatic, BUT before she puts on the top layer she'll have to add something …

He/she puts on the stole

> Sometimes it was worn like this. *(put it on priest-fashion)*
> But *Mother/Father N* wears it like this ... *(he/she puts it on deacon-fashion)*
> Does that remind you of anything?
> Yup, the towel.
> It looked even more like a towel in the fourth century.
> Why did they do that?
> Well, one thing might give you a clue.
> One of the ministers was called a diakonos.

Circle the word 'diakonos'

To the deacon

New deacon
Preacher

> I'm guessing you were taught Greek; what does diakonos mean?
> It means a servant.
> Exactly. Diakonoi were servants of the Church, servants of the bishop and the people of God, and they wore this towel to remind them of their status.
> So under all the super clothes – and Christians made sure their top cloak looked very good indeed – there was this stole, to remind them they were servants.
> If the diakonos really *was* a gentleman, he wouldn't have liked wearing a towel very much. But then he'd have remembered the story in the Gospel. The one when Jesus rose from the supper table, and wrapped a towel round Himself and washed His disciples' feet. Jesus didn't mind being a servant – He came to earth to serve us.
> In the Christian faith it's a great thing to be a servant.
>
> Do you know what the Pope is called? The servant of the servants of God.
> We still have servants in the Church, and we call them by the old name of diakonos or deacon. This morning we welcome our new deacon *(Mother/Father N)* to St *(name of your church)*. *(He/she)* is very lucky to be a deacon – and we're very lucky to have one.

Start a clap

INTRODUCING A NEW PRIEST

Ad lib about Petertide, it being the time of year when people are ordained as priests or deacons

  And this Petertide (or whenever it was) *Mother/Father N* was priested. That is, they were already a deacon – and now they're a priest as well.

YOKES

  OK, well obviously we're going to talk about priests – but first we're going to talk about carrying things
  Do any of you give your mum a hand in the supermarket?

(See what they say, bring the subject round to supermarket trolleys, and putting things in the car)

  What do you think people did before there were cars?
  They carried everything about, in wheelbarrows, or on donkeys, or – more usually – on their backs. You can't imagine what a faff it was.

Pull out your 'yoke', add the bundles, and give an impressive demo, helped by a child

  That's why people loved it when Jesus said *(pull out the Bible)* 'my yoke is easy, my burden is light'. *(Matthrew 11.30)*
  Mind you, He didn't say He was going to get rid of yokes. But *His* yoke is easy and, unlike ordinary yokes, it keeps your hands free.

Over to the new priest. Recap on the sequence above – see page 00 – on what a fourth century gent wore, and how they dressed as a deacon. Help them get into their amice, alb and girdle

  But now *Mother/Father N* is a priest – and they wear their stole like this …

The priest puts on his/her stole

  And no more snazzy dalmatics, *he/she* wears a toga – or a chasuble as we call it nowadays.

Bring it to him/her and comment on its weight

New priest Yes, I say a special prayer when I put it on.

He/she takes the chasuble and says

  O Lord, who has said, 'My yoke is sweet and my burden light', grant that I may so carry it as to merit thy grace. Amen.

And then puts it over his/her head

Preacher So the chasuble is a yoke.
Does it feel heavy? Does the job feel heavy?

Leave it up to the new priest here. (They usually say, 'Well of course it feels heavy, but Jesus' yoke is light because He makes it so.' Sometimes they go on to talk about the grace of ordination – the way that the sacrament empowers you to do your new job)

Let's look at the chasuble more closely. *(especially if it's a Roman one – see diagram below)*
Does it keep your hands free? Do you work with your hands?

The priest ad libs and demonstrates some of the gestures of Mass – the 'orans' position for prayer perhaps, or spreading the hands over the elements, taking bread, blessing, breaking, elevating, blessing kids

Preacher So you see that a new priest may look like a Roman gentleman – but they work with their hands. In fact, God trusts Himself to *Mother/Father N's* hands. When you feel *his/her* hands on your head, you're actually feeling Jesus' hands, who is using *Mother/Father N* to bless you.

You could ask the priest the journalistic 'How does that feel?'
At all events, you agree that it's wonderful that God can use ordinary people like Father/Mother N and use their hands to bless His people

Thank God for priests.

Script 30   The Assumption
(15 August)

*Any of the Gospels appointed for the feast day on 15 August.
It's often the account of the Visitation, Luke 1.39–45.*

> **THEME**
>
> We believe that the Virgin Mary is now in Heaven where she prays for us to her Son and, from a very early time, the Church has also believed that she, like Elijah and Enoch, was taken up, bodily, into Heaven.[47] Mary's 'Assumption' is a major holiday in Europe,[48] and the Church of England also honours the day, 15 August, though we hedge our bets on what we think about her bodily Assumption by calling it a 'Feast of Our Lady'. Anglo-catholic churches naturally call this feast by its traditional name and this session gives a straightforward account of the Assumption. Then it moves into story-telling mode. Mary's passing is not recorded in Scripture, but we're lucky enough to have plenty of legends. The one we've chosen is about St Thomas, who managed to miss the Assumption, but got a consolation prize. Legend or not, the story makes the important point that Mary went up as her ordinary self, with all her habitual kindness, thoughtfulness, and (apparently) in her normal clothes.

---

47 Interestingly, there are no, absolutely no, relics of Our Lady. Nobody, not even the hundreds of con men who made fake relics, ever dared to suggest they'd got the smallest bone of Our Lady's body. The tradition that her body was taken straight to Heaven is so early that the relic merchants knew that they hadn't got a chance.

48 It is a major feast for the Orthodox Church as well. They call it the 'Dormition of the Mother of God' because – though they believe Our Lady was taken bodily into Heaven – they emphasize that she died a normal death first. This also appears to be the Roman Catholic position, affirmed by John Paul II in 1997.

Script 30 – The Assumption (15 August)

SET UP

- A1 flip-chart.
- Marker pens, black, red and yellow.
- Pictures 30.1–30.12 from www.canterburypress.co.uk/downloads.
- A leather belt.
- Place the St Thomas story below in a folder, to make it look like a story book.

ADDRESS

Ad lib welcome. Talk through the name of the feast day – the Assumption of Our Lady

> Does anyone know what that means?

Establish that it is the day Mary died and went to Heaven

> Yup, well, we'll all going to get to Heaven one day, but the Church tells us that Mary was *assumed* into Heaven.
> Does anyone know what that means?

(Take anything that comes. Unpack it and talk through the timeline picture, drawn following the template provided to make up the picture)

> OK, well here's a timeline. *(draw a horizontal line across the chart)*
> And here's where we are …

Put in the year number about halfway along the line

> in time.

Write 'Time' under the line

> And here's God …

Stick on Picture 30.1 of Jesus

> outside time.

Write 'Outside Time' round Jesus

> OK, so one of you kids is on the line (*Picture 30.2*).

Stick kid on the year number

> And in about 100 years' time

Write 2120 a little way along the time line

> you'll be incredibly old, and it'll be time for you to leave the planet. So you'll die, and your body will get buried.

Be very matter-of-fact about this and draw a tombstone with a cheery RIP (Picture 30.3). Children are not usually bothered

>Then nobody quite knows what happens but, as God will be looking after us, it's obviously going to be fine and *(draw a line above the timeline right to the end)* at the End of Time …

Write 'The End'

>God will make everything new and give us new bodies.

Add yellow rays round the kid and move to 'The End'

>We'll be in Heaven, with Jesus, and our new bodies for ever.

Swoosh the resurrected kid up from the timeline and place him/her beside Jesus

>But some people don't have to wait until the End of Time. Way back …

Put the date 850 BC on the timeline

>the prophet Elijah …

Stick on Elijah (Picture 30.4)

>went up to Heaven, just as he was, in a fiery chariot *(Picture 30.5)*.

Swoosh him up

>And we believe that the Virgin Mary, round about AD 50…

Write AD 50 and place Mary on the timeline (Picture 30.6)

>died, and was buried *(put on an open tomb, Picture 30.7)*, but didn't hang around in her tomb and went straight up to Heaven, like Elijah, in her ordinary body.

Swoosh Mary up to Jesus and place her by her Son

>And of course that's where she is, right now, this moment.
>It's why we can ask her to pray for us.
>When people go to Heaven like that, we say they are *assumed*.
>God draws them up to be with Him, just as they are.
>So today is the Feast of the Assumption of Our Lady, and the church fills up with flowers and gold vestments *(adapt to local custom)* and it's all very cheerful. In fact, it's a good time to tell stories – so I'm going to tell you one now.

Move from homily-mode to story-telling mode. You could perhaps sit among the kids, or grab a stool, and get a trusty helper to put up the pictures on cue. Read the following script from what appears to be a story book, and have the belt to hand.

Script 30 – The Assumption (15 August)

ST THOMAS

When Jesus was alive He knew a couple of twins. They were called Timothy and Thomas. (*Picture 30.8*)

They were almost impossible to tell apart, but it didn't matter, because you never saw them together. If Tim was on a bus, then Tom was the one who had just missed it. If Tim was in the cinema, then Tom was outside looking for his ticket.

Tom was late for everything – he missed his meals, he missed goals, he even managed to miss the Resurrection. (*Picture 30.9*)

But it didn't matter because everyone was fond of him. Jesus loved him – and so did Jesus' mother, the Virgin Mary. And once Jesus had gone back to Heaven, Mary, Thomas and the others used to hang round with each other, to break bread, and pray.

And one day Mary told them it was time for her to die and go to Heaven to be with her Son.

Sure enough, about a week later, Tim found Tom and said that Mary had died and her funeral was that afternoon.

'This afternoon?!' said Thomas.

'Yes,' said Timothy, 'don't be late!'

'Right!' said Thomas. And he dashed off – but he couldn't find his sandals, or his key, or his bus pass.

So he had to run to the burial ground – and when he got there it was all over. He saw a tomb, and his mates, but as he ran up he saw them all looking into the sky. (*Picture 30.10*)

'What's going on?' said Thomas.

'Look!' said Peter. 'There she is! Mary's going straight to Heaven …'

'WHAT!?' said Thomas, and *he* looked up and, sure enough, there was Mary rising above them, looking completely ordinary. (*Picture 30.11*)

It was amazing, but Thomas thought, 'I never said goodbye to her, I've missed the boat again …' And at that moment, Mary looked down and smiled. 'Goodbye, Thomas!' she cried and, because he looked so downcast, 'Here! Catch!' And she threw something down.

Add belt to picture (Picture 30.12)

> Can you see what it is?
> **(Her belt)**
> 'Take my belt to remember me by,' said Mary. 'And I'll pray to my Son for you.'
> Thomas caught the belt – it was like this *(produce the leather belt)*, made of leather and quite ordinary. And as he pulled it …

Pull the belt with your hands

> he knew that Mary had been as real as her belt, and really had gone to Heaven just as she was.
> So Thomas went home a very happy man. He had Our Lady's belt, and whenever he saw it he asked her to pray for him (*Picture 30.12*) and he used to say to his mates, 'It's the people who turn up last who often get the prize!'

Shut the book

> Well, that story is not in the Bible. It's a legend.
> Which bits sound correct?

Call up a reliable kid or server for this and, using a red marker pen, circle the pictures that we believe are true

> OK, well St Thomas is real. *(circle Tom)*
> And he *did* have a twin. *(circle Tim)*
> I don't think he ever ran for a bus though – does anyone know why?
> **(They weren't invented)**
> Yup, but Mary did go to Heaven in her body. *(circle the Assumption)*
> And Thomas, and his mates, and Christians ever since, have asked her to pray for us.

Circle the picture of Thomas praying

> He had the right idea – let's do that too.

Finish with intercessions (you'll find some online) or a Hail Mary

Script 31   St Michael and All Angels
(29 September)

Matthew 18.1–10

> **THEME**
>
> Who is St Michael? And what are angels? This session introduces children to the reality of angels, conscious of the twin dangers of making them sound like space aliens or fairies.

SET UP

- Angel prop box containing:
- Three sets of angel wings; you can get cheap ones online, go for fake feathers rather than butterfly wings.
- Put the wings on top of everything else.
- A child-size white alb, or plain white nightdress.
- White T-shirt.
- A couple of torches.
- A green T-shirt or jumper.
- Plastic armour plus helmet and sword.
- A large Bible, marked up (see below).
- Three kids prepared to dress up on cue.

Optional

- An image of St Michael. If you go for an image from the internet, download a full-length one, with dragon. There are fairly cheap plastic statues of him available.

Script 31 – St Michael and All Angels (29 September)

ADDRESS

Ad lib into today being the Feast of St Michael and All Angels

> I think the first thing to do is sort out who we are talking about.
> Does anyone know who St Michael is?

(Take anything that comes, you may have to give the answer yourself)

> He is the Captain of the Angels.
> But what is an angel? *(make this rhetorical)*
> OK, where do angels live?
> **(In Heaven)**
> Yup, you're right, they live with God in Heaven.
> What do they look like? *(another rhetorical question)*
> OK, here's an angel kit box – how about coming up and pulling out something that will make you look like an angel …

With any luck, a kid will pull out a pair of wings

> Brilliant! If you ever see a picture of an angel, it will have wings.

Refer if possible to any visible picture or statue in your church

> Do angels actually have wings?

(Take any answer)

> Well, we don't know. Artists give them wings to show how fast they are, and because they seem to come down from the sky.
> And actually some of the angels we read about in the Bible seem to be covered with wings.
> There's a famous moment when the prophet Isaiah sees angels in the Temple

Turn to Isaiah 6.1–3 in the Bible; whatever version you use, establish that God was surrounded by angels

> Listen to this:
> 'With two they covered their feet, and with two they covered their face, and with two they flew.'
> How many wings is that? *(count them off)*
> With **two** they covered their feet,
> and with **two** they covered their face,
> and with **two** they flew.
> How many's that?
> **(Six!)**
> Six wings each!
> Can we try that?

Script 31 – St Michael and All Angels (29 September)

See if you can arrange three pairs of wings on a child

> Hmm, it's pretty difficult – how about flying?
> Nope, we can't do that either.
> Angels are more tricky than you think.

Turn to Daniel 10.4–6

> Here's the moment when the prophet Ezekiel saw St Michael himself.
> Let's see what he looked like:

> On the twenty-fourth day of the first month, as I was standing on the bank of the great river (that is, the Tigris), I saw a man clothed in linen, with a belt of gold from Uphaz around his waist. His body was like beryl, his face like lightning, his eyes like flaming torches, his arms and legs like the gleam of burnished bronze, and the sound of his words like the roar of a multitude.

> We can do that. Anyone like to be St Michael?
> OK … clothed in linen.

Put the alb/nightdress on the kid

> What next?
> 'His body was like beryl'
> OK, beryl is green …

Put the green garment on the kid

> 'His face like lightning'.

Double-take at kid

> I think we'll skip that bit …
> 'his eyes like flaming torches'
> Well, we've got some torches *(produce them)* – Hmm, I don't see how we're going to make that work …
> 'and the sound of his words like the roar of a multitude'.

Look at the kid

> We just can't do it, can we? Nice try!
> Surely there are more simple angels – ah, what about this …

Read out the appearances to women at the Tomb and the young man in white clothes

> So angels can look ordinary …

Ask another kid forward

> no wings, no lightning, just a youngster in white clothes.

He/she puts on the white T-shirt

> Why do you think angels appear in such different ways? *(rhetorical)*
> Well, the answer is right here, in church.
> Everybody here has got a Guardian Angel.

Turn to a kid you can trust to pick up a cue

> *Name*, come up here will you?
> Bring your Guardian Angel with you …

Stand the child a little apart from the 'angels' in costume

> Right, so here's *Name*, with his/her Guardian Angel.

To the kid

> Which side is it on, *Name*?

The child is unlikely to know – whatever they say, reply

> OK, but I can't see it.
> Can anyone see *Name's* Guardian Angel?
> (**No**)
> No, and there's a simple reason for that.
> Angels don't have bodies like us, they are spirits and completely invisible – to us at any rate.
> The church is full of Guardian Angels this morning, and we can't see any of them.
> But if God sends an angel to talk to us, then the angel makes sure it can be seen. They look like a human being and they wear what they think will be appropriate for their message.
> The angels Isaiah saw in the Temple

Go over to the kid with three pairs of wings

> wanted to look holy, and slightly different, so they covered themselves with wings.
> And the angel who appeared at the Tomb …

Go over to the kid in white

> didn't want to frighten the women, so he looked like an ordinary young man.

Go over to the kid in green

> And St Michael had a marvellous time working out what he was going to wear to meet Ezekiel. Fortunately, he often turns up in another costume …

To the kid

> How about getting that stuff off

He/she might need some help

> Can anyone remember who St Michael is?
> **(The Captain of the Angels)**
> Brilliant, and as the Captain of the Angels we often see him in full armour, fighting evil.

OPTIONAL EXTRA ON ST MICHAEL

If you've got an image of St Michael in your church, refer to it now; the dragon at his feet represents evil

> People often get St Michael muddled up with St George, because both of them are in full armour and are fighting a dragon. But if you look carefully you can always spot the difference. St George is a man, whereas St Michael isn't human at all – how do we know that?
> **(He's got wings)**
> Yes – the wings, a dead give-away.

BACK TO SCRIPT

To the kid playing St Michael

> Have we got any armour in that box?
> How about putting it on? *(He/she does – don't forget the wings)*
> So there you are: three visible angels in front of us and …

Do an improbable count of the congregation

> at least *Number (the apparent total of your congregation)* angels in church this morning.
> Jesus said that our Guardian Angels see our Father's face in Heaven.
> They are brilliant people to pray to.

Script 32   All Souls
(31 October)

John 5.19–25 or John 6.37–40

LAYING GHOSTS

It seems unlikely that any family service will concentrate on All Souls, when the glorious All Saints Day is the day after. However, your church may be dedicated to All Souls, or you might feel that, what with the popularity of pumpkins and Trick or Treat, the children need a Christian take on Hallowe'en. This session takes the medieval line that the best way to deal with a devil is to laugh at him.

SET UP

- Hallowe'en props; your local toy shop will have masses: go for skulls and scythes (these are useful props all the year round), something ghostly, plus some assorted broomsticks and witches' hats. Ridiculous props – the sort that glow in the dark – are ideal. Don't worry about the kids' sensibilities, it's the adults who'll look alarmed: even so, a very bloody Frankenstein mask is probably not a good idea.
- Some Hallowe'en cakes or decorations for cakes – marzipan spiders, etc.
- A1 flip-chart with three calendar pages written on it (see template).
- Make a pumpkin lantern and have a candle ready.

Script 32 – All Souls (31 October)

ADDRESS

HALLOWE'EN SESSION

Produce the pumpkin lantern – without a candle

> OK, what's this?
> **(A pumpkin!)**
> And why have I got one?
> **(It's Hallowe'en)**

Get the kids to tell you about Hallowe'en, how they dress up, what they decorate cakes with. Bring out props as the kids mention them, then muck around – they love a sudden swoop of the plastic scythe

> That sounds really scary – are you scared of Hallowe'en?
> **(NO! – just a bit)**

React to one of the props yourself

> I think this one is horrible!
> Why do you suppose we do all this? *(rhetorical question)*
> Well, this is the month in which we think about the dead.

(Some kids like to be told that November is the Month of the Dead)

> It's a time when we think about the Saints in Heaven, and the Holy Souls – that's the people who are dead – who are on their way to Heaven.
> We remember them on two days:
> All Saints Day on 1 November.
> All Souls Day on 2 November

Move over to the flip-chart and put the 1 and 2 on the appropriate 'calendar pages'

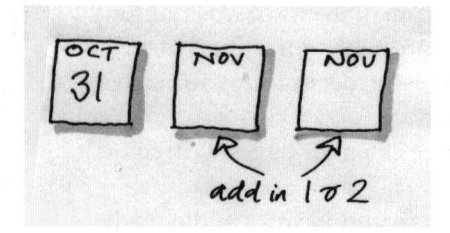

> OCT 31 | NOV | NOV
> *add in 1 & 2*

In the old days 'All Saints' was called 'All Hallows'.

Write up the word 'Hallow'

> What does 'Hallow' mean? *(rhetorical)*
> OK, can you say the first line of the Lord's Prayer?
> (**Our Father, Who art in Heaven, Hallowed be thy name ...**')
> Stop there! 'Hallow' means 'Holy'.
> And a hallow is a holy person, a saint.
>
> Now on really big feasts we start to get excited on the day before, so we have 'Christmas', and the day before we have 'Christmas Evening' – which we shorten to 'Christmas Eve'.
> People used to feel the same about the day before All Hallows, *(add '31' to the first calendar page)*
> so the day before, All Souls, used to be called 'Hallows Evening'.
> And that got shortened to ... *(add 'evening' to Hallow, cross out the 'v' and 'ing' with a red pen)*
> Yup – Hallowe'en.

HALLOWE'EN

> Now of course the holy Saints and Souls are fine – they're not scary at all. But the bits of death that are left behind here on Earth – you know, skeletons, and ghosts and stuff – are kinda frightening. But if you look at them closely *(stare at a skull, preferably the ridiculous luminous sort)* – they just look silly. So to get over our fright, we laugh at them.
> I think that's a good idea.
> But just remember – inside every grinning pumpkin ...

Bring the pumpkin back

> there's a candle.

Light a candle and ask a kid to help you take the top off and place the candle

> God's light shines through everything, especially through Death – and certainly through Pumpkins!

Script 33   Jigsaw Man
(All Saints Day – 1 November)

The Gospel is normally one of the versions of the Beatitudes.
Matthew 5.1–12

THEME

Jesus' list of blessed people in Matthew 5 gives us an idea of what a saint is like. This session describes a saint as a complete human being. This is done by introducing the children to the idea that evil is a lack of something, a hole. Most of us aren't quite complete – we've got empty spaces within us. Together we fill in the gaps in a human being by putting together a large jigsaw and, when we've got to the end, we've got a nice ordinary human being – a saint. Small children will like filling in the jigsaw, but this session works better with older kids.

SET UP

- A1 flip-chart.
- Blu Tack or similar.
- Pictures 33.1–33.2b from www.canterburypress.co.uk/downloads. Picture 33.2b is the jigsaw pieces to be cut out and stuck with Blu Tack on to the gaps in the jigsaw in Picture 33.2a. Have them prepared with bits of Blu Tack for the address.

GOSPEL   Matthew 5.1–12

ADDRESS

Ad lib that today is All Saints Day; see if the children know the saint your church is dedicated to[49]

> Yep, that's our saint. Do we know any others?

---

[49] If you are dedicated to the Holy Trinity or the Holy Cross, go straight on to the images of saints in your church.

Script 33 – Jigsaw Man (All Saints Day – 1 November)

Use any pictures or glass windows or statues to hand, keep it snappy

What do we know about saints?

This might be too much for the kids, but establish a couple of things – they love Jesus, they live in Heaven, and home in on the fact that …

They are good.
And today in the Gospel we heard Jesus describing saints, saying how marvellous – how blessed – it is to be good.
Now I've got good news for you; Jesus thought it was blessed to be a little child as well *(look up at the congregation)* so here at the front we've got a whole bunch of saints – or nearly saints.
But sometimes people get worried about saints; they say, 'Oh they're *too* good, I'll never be a saint.' But God doesn't think so. He's expecting us all to be saints.
And this is why …

What stops us being good? *(probably a rhetorical question)*
Well, we get cross, or we do something unkind, or make someone unhappy, and then everything gets messed up and we know we've done something wrong.
And the interesting thing is, why do we do it?
It might be because we're hungry – we feel as if we've got a hole in our tummy *(hand on your tum)*; or perhaps we don't feel anyone loves us – we've got a gap in our heart *(hand on your heart)*; or maybe we feel we've got so many empty spaces inside we need to fill them up with *things (clench your hands and arms in a 'grab' gesture)* – our things, other people's things, anything …

Picture 33.1   Look, here's an ordinary human being …
That's how God made him – super happy with a loving heart and a happy face.
He looks OK, doesn't he? That's what he sees in the mirror.
But God sees something different. He sees that things aren't always as they should be.

Picture 33.2a Same chap, but now he's a jigsaw, with several bits missing

The poor chap has got lots of bits missing *(point out the gaps as you go through)*
That smile disappeared when he felt his mum didn't love him,
and that bit went when he got bullied,
and that gap happened when he didn't have enough to eat,

and that hole happened when he was so unhappy he stopped believing in God.

It's horrible to have gaps like that. Somebody who has a pain inside often lashes out, or grabs things, or hurts people, all that stuff.

But God doesn't think a person like that is bad; he or she is just empty and unhappy.

So God looks at a chap like this and thinks:

I'll send him someone to love, so he'll get his heart back.

From now on children begin to find pieces cut out from Picture 33.2b and fill in the jigsaw as you say:

And perhaps he'll start thinking about other people.
And stop being frightened.
And forgive people.
And love them.
And get to know Me.
And by the end – wonderful – he's OK, he's just the way I made him.

Reserve the smile piece to the end and put it in now

A complete human being
Do you know what we call that?
(**A saint**)
Yup, a saint is a complete human being – and that's just what we're going to be.

Script 34 Christ the King

John 18.33–37 or Luke 23.35–43

> **THEME**
>
> There are many ways of approaching this feast. The Gospels direct us to Christ on Earth as the Servant King or the Hidden King but, after His Ascension, the Early Church celebrated Christ as Pantocrator – the King of the Universe. This seems a fitting way to finish the church year.

SET UP

- Piece of plasticine.
- Blow-drier.
- Ping pong ball – colour it green and blue with marker pens; it is supposed to represent the world.
- Two white ping pong balls.
- Extension lead to a power point.
- You are going to suspend three ping pong balls in the air stream of the blow-drier – practise beforehand.
- Inflatable globe (you can get these for £2 on the internet at the time of writing).
- Picture of Christ as the Pantocrator – an easy image to find on the internet.

ADDRESS

> Today we are celebrating the Feast of Christ the King.
> It's the end of the church year, and a great place to finish.
> But what is Christ the King *of*?

(Take all answers – the Earth, the Church, the world. Establish He is the King of the Universe, of everything there is.)

> How do we know that?
> Well, to start with, we know that God made the world – so it's not surprising He's King of it. But there's more to being a King than that.

Script 34 – Christ the King

>You see, if you make something, you have to look after it …
>I'll make a world.

Take some plasticine and make a globe of it

>There we are – a nice plasticine world. Much smaller than me. I think I'll throw it into space and let it get on with life.

Toss the globe in the air and look with dismay as it falls to the ground

>How did that happen?

Pick it up

>It's got a bit bashed.

Mould it a bit and cup it in your hands

>If I want this little world to keep going, I'm obviously going to have to look after it better than that.
>Well, God made this world – let's have a look at it.

Pull out your inflatable globe – establish which way up it should go; find the UK

>Yup, God made Britain. Any other countries?

Find a few more – Australia, the USA, Italy, an African country, etc.

>And He made the sea, and our planet, and He set it off, orbiting round the sun.

Hold the globe up and move it in a circle as you say this

>And the interesting thing is, it's gone on orbiting …
>Let's see if this can orbit by itself …

Do so

>Oh, all it did was bounce. Thank goodness I'm not the King of the world …
>You see, looking after things is more than just getting them going. It's like having a new baby. You can't say to the baby – 'OK, you've been made. You're alive, get on with it. Good luck!' The baby needs you to look after it. To feed it and – this is really important – to love it.
>God looks after the world all the time.
>It's a bit like this …

Get your blow-drier going on its lowest setting, turn it up so you get a vertical stream, and hold up your blue and green ball

> Right, this is the world. It's very small and, as you can see, it's swirly green and blue – that's what it looks like in space. And somehow it's got to stay in space and not go bouncing off anywhere. So …

Place your ping pong ball carefully in the stream of air. It will (when you get the hang of it) bob around at its own level. If you get it wrong, don't worry, retrieve it and try again saying

> I am more and more convinced that it's a good thing I'm not God …

Once the ball is safely bobbing

> But of course the Earth isn't the only thing God made – He made the sun and the other planets, and the stars and the galaxies, and they've all got to keep going. Let's add another planet …

Add your second ball

> Do you think we could add a third?

Add another. All three will bob around in the stream of air

> What's keeping them up?
> **(The air)**
> Yes, we can't see the air – but it's holding the balls, keeping them lively – look at them bounce – and safe and cheerful. The air is sustaining them.
> And that's how God rules the universe – He doesn't boss it around, or leave it to get on with life by itself – He loves it and sustains it. And He goes on doing it. That stream of air is happening now, so the balls are safe. But someone like me might get bored with this drier and – turn it off!

Turn off the blow-drier – let the kids scramble for the balls

> But God never gets bored. He loved us when He made us, and He loves us right now. Let's be ready to thank Him and greet Him as our King as we come to the Altar.

Script 34 – Christ the King

OPTIONAL SECTION ON THE PANTOCRATOR

The early Christians used to call today the Feast of Christ the Pantocrator.

Write it up, and draw a line between 'Panto' and 'crator'

Panto means 'All'[50] and 'crator' is usually translated as 'powerful' or 'King' – Jesus the all-powerful. But you could translate crator as 'sustainer'. Christ is the sustainer of all.

Here's a picture of Jesus as the Pantocrator …

Show them an image of the Pantocrator. The one at Cefalu in Sicily is particularly magnificent. Go through the image.

The Pantocrator

© Andreas Wahra
https://commons.wikimedia.org/wiki/File:Cefalu_Christus_Pantokrator.jpg

Jesus is blessing us with His right hand and holding the book of the Gospels in His left. The IC and XC stand for Jesus Christ (in this sort of Greek, I = J and C = S, X = Ch and C is S again). So it's an abbreviation: JesuS CHriSt. Behind Jesus is the gold of Heaven. He is placed in the ceiling over the altar and looks down blessing His people.

---

50 A theatrically alert congregation might be interested to know that Pantomime means a show in which everything (Panto) is mimed (mime), or at least is very physical and slap-stick.

Script 35 The Rich Fool
(Harvest)

Luke 12.16–21

> **THEME**
>
> This session homes in on God's indifference to arithmetic when He showers His gifts upon us.

SET UP

- A bread stick.
- A tube of Smarties or a packet of chocolate buttons.
- Some large bags of potatoes, enough to weigh a kid down.
- Set a chair on the sanctuary steps.
- A child or teenager to be the farmer, go through the script with them beforehand.
- The session assumes you have some sort of Harvest display in church.

ADDRESS

>   We've just heard the story of the rich farmer.
>   He had loads of food.
>   Let's see what he did with it. *Name*, would you be the farmer for me?

The farmer steps forward

>   Right, so this chap was a potato farmer and he had a really good harvest.

Indicate the pile of potatoes

>   Look at that, tons of spuds –
>   Bet you don't know how many you've got?

Farmer	Yes I do! *(does a fast and improbable count)* I've got one thousand and thirty-two.
Preacher	Impressive! Well, he stacked the whole lot up …

Stack them up on the farmer's open arms – do some patter: 'Heavy, aren't they?' 'Do you think you can manage another one?' 'Do you really want the last 32?' (YES!)

and packed them away in his barn.

The farmer walks across to the chair and packs the potatoes underneath

Then he sat on the whole lot.

The farmer sits down

He was very pleased with himself.

The farmer folds his/her arms

And he said, 'Great, I won't have to do any work for a bit. I'll just stay at home, and eat all this food, and have a good time …'

Turn to the farmer

Just a minute – aren't you going to invite your mates round?

Farmer	No!
Preacher	Or give a bag of spuds to the poor?

(Substitute the name of a local Homeless charity if you've got one)

Farmer	No way!
Preacher	OK, well, have it your own way –

To the other kids

And that night God spoke to the farmer and said, 'You fool! Supposing you died tonight – who'd get your food then?'
Well, *Name (the child playing the farmer)* isn't going to die tonight, but the farmer did.

Farmer dies a very impressive panto death

So he never ate his potatoes – and they went to other people after all.
Why did God call him 'a fool'?

(Take any answer – they'll probably hover round a censorious 'He should have shared his food')

Yup, he should have shared his stuff.
But, you know, I have a sort of sympathy with that farmer.

Script 35 – The Rich Fool (Harvest)

Of course, he was very greedy – but it can be quite tough learning to share.
Look – here's a bread stick. *(produce it)*
It's my bread stick, and I'm looking forward to eating it.
Anyone here like bread sticks?

Look fed up as the kids put up their hands

Oh, blow. That's a pity – do you think I should share it?
(Yes)

Break off some bits of the bread stick and hand them out. Look with dismay at what's left

Hey, the bread stick's got smaller! How did that happen?

Let them tell you

Yeah, that's the trouble with sharing –
It's even worse if it's Smarties …

Pour some Smarties into your hand

I've got *(do a count)* ten Smarties here. Anyone like one?

Dish them out, one by one – it shouldn't be a free for all. Do a grumpy patter, 'Oh no, another one gone …'

Rats, I'm down to five! Every time I share my food I lose half of it.

Pocket the Smarties

I think sharing is really difficult.
Why does God want us to do it?

(A rhetorical question, but take any answers – establish that He wants us to be kind and generous)

Well, He may want us to be kind and generous – but how does He help us do it?
I'll tell you – by giving us the harvest!

Turn to the harvest display

Look at all that stuff …
It was grown by farmers, and put in packets by people in factories – but who actually made it?
(God)
Yup, He made those potatoes – let's put them with the harvest display – and He made that pumpkin, and all these apples …

Script 35 – The Rich Fool (Harvest)

Hold up a tin of baked beans

> I bet God knows every bean in this tin.
> He knows exactly how many apples and grapes He made this year – and He could easily say:
> 'Just a minute! I'm down a couple of million strawberries! Where did *they* go?'

(Ad lib after any church fete: 'I can tell you that, at least a million went at our church fete last month …')

> But the great thing is God gives and gives – and He *doesn't* count, which is a bit of luck for us.
> So this harvest, let's thank God for all His gifts, and try to be like Him.
> He gave me these Smarties to eat, and to share …

Pull them out again

> How many have I got? Five …
> OK, four for my friends *(dish them out)* and one for myself.

Eat it

> Thank you, God.

Appendixes

Eucharistic Prayer H

Lord be with you *(or)* The Lord is here.
And also with you.
His Spirit is with us.

Lift up your hearts.
We lift them to the Lord.

Let us give thanks to the Lord our God.
It is right to give thanks and praise.

It is right to praise you, Father, Lord of all creation;
in your love you made us for yourself.

When we turned away
you did not reject us,
but came to meet us in your Son.
You embraced us as your children
and welcomed us to sit and eat with you.

In Christ you shared our life
that we might live in him and he in us.
He opened his arms of love upon the cross
and made for all the perfect sacrifice for sin.

On the night he was betrayed,
at supper with his friends
he took bread, and gave you thanks;
he broke it and gave it to them, saying:
Take, eat; this is my body which is given for you;
do this in remembrance of me.
Father, we do this in remembrance of him:
his body is the bread of life.

Eucharistic Prayer H

At the end of supper, taking the cup of wine,
he gave you thanks, and said:
Drink this, all of you; this is my blood of the new covenant,
which is shed for you for the forgiveness of sins;
do this in remembrance of me.
Father, we do this in remembrance of him:
his blood is shed for all.

As we proclaim his death and celebrate his rising in glory,
send your Holy Spirit that this bread and this wine
may be to us the body and blood of your dear Son.
As we eat and drink these holy gifts
make us one in Christ, our risen Lord.

With your whole Church throughout the world
we offer you this sacrifice of praise
and lift our voice to join the eternal song of heaven:

Holy, holy, holy Lord,
God of power and might,
Heaven and earth are full of your glory.
Hosanna in the highest.

The service continues with the Lord's Prayer.

Common Worship: Services and Prayers for the Church of England, 2011, Church House Publishing.

Children's Liturgy for Good Friday

SET UP

- The nave, altar and the area where the children sit should be lit – the rest of the church, dim.
- Set the children's processional cross at the back, plus two candlesticks.
- Set the objects of the Passion on the benches at the sides of the altar.
- Have three children ready to bring the cross slowly in procession.
- Ask the Sunday school leaders to find children to bring the objects up (when cued). They are:
    1. Club and sword.
    2. Basin and towel.
    3. Crown of thorns and purple robe.
    4. The processional cross.
    5. Hammer and nails.
    6. Sponge and reed.
    7. Hymns from the *New English Hymnal*.

THE LITURGY

The priest welcomes the children and draws their attention to the unveiled crosses in church

>Why are the crosses unveiled?

Take all answers and proceed

>Today is Good Friday, the day Jesus died for us on the Cross.
>We remember that as we make the **Sign of the Cross.**
>
>**+ In the Name of the Father …**

The Arrest in the Garden

>The Good Friday story starts on the night before, in a garden. Jesus was praying among the olive trees, when He saw a crowd approaching – with these weapons.

A couple of children come forward with the club and the sword. They stand in front of the altar as the following passage is read. After the reading they place them on the altar; you follow the same format for all the objects and readings

Reader A crowd with swords and clubs came into the garden, with Jesus' friend, Judas, leading them. And Judas came up to Jesus, and said, 'Hail master!'
And kissed Him.
Jesus said, 'My friend, what are you doing here?'
And to the crowd He said, 'Do you think I am a robber? Do you need swords and clubs? But this is your hour and the power of darkness!'
And they arrested Him – while all His disciples ran away.

The priest Jesus had done nothing wrong, he was ambushed and hurried away to a secret trial. There are many people in the world who have been sent to prison unfairly, just like Him – let us kneel and pray for them.

A child Let us pray for all prisoners.
That God will hear the prayers of all those who cry to Him.
And bless and comfort those who have been unjustly imprisoned.
Amen.

The Romans

Two children bring forward a bowl of water and a towel

Reader Jesus was brought for trial before Pilate the Roman Governor.
Pilate asked Him, 'Are you the King of the Jews?'
Jesus said to him, 'Did somebody else tell you that?'
And Pilate said, 'Listen, I am not a Jew. Your own people want to kill you. What have you done?'
Jesus said, 'I *am* a King – but not in the way you think.'
Then Pilate said to the people round about, 'What shall I do with Jesus?'
And they answered, 'Let Him be crucified!'
And he said, 'Why? What evil has He done?'
But they shouted all the more, 'Let Him be crucified!'
So when Pilate saw he was gaining nothing, but rather a riot was beginning, he took water and washed his hands, and said, 'I am innocent of the blood of this good man; see to it yourselves.'

The priest (washing his hands in the bowl)

> When Pilate washed his hands he was saying, 'It's not *my* fault. Look! My hands are clean!'
> Pilate was a Roman and a pagan and it seems that he didn't know God well enough to stand up for what he knew was right. Let us kneel and pray for people without faith.

Child
> Let us pray for all those who do not know God, or believe in Jesus, That God the Holy Spirit will lead them to the truth,
> **Amen.**

Jesus is mocked

Two children hold the crown of thorns and the robe

Reader
> The soldiers that led Jesus away clothed Him in a purple robe and, plaiting a crown of thorns, they put it on His head. And they saluted Him and said, 'Hail! King of the Jews!'
> And they struck His head with a reed, and spat upon Him and knelt before Him – and, when they had finished jeering at Him, they stripped off the purple robe and put His own clothes on Him; and led Him out to be crucified.

The crown of thorns is placed on the altar, the robe is draped in front

The priest
> The Romans mocked Jesus for being the King of the Jews. They thought He was being stupid and they began to bully Him. Nobody believed He really was a King – the Romans didn't, the Jews didn't, even we sometimes forget. Let us kneel and pray for all Jews and Christians.

A child
> Let us pray for the Jewish people,
> the first to hear the Word of God.
> Dear Lord, we ask that all your people, Jews and Christians, may grow in love for each other and for you.
> **Amen.**

Jesus carries His Cross

An adult takes three children to the back of the church, to set up the Procession

Reader	The soldiers took Jesus, and He went out, bearing His own Cross, to the place of a skull, which is called in Hebrew, Golgotha. And many people followed him, especially women who wept and lamented for Him. But Jesus turned to them and said, 'Daughters of Jerusalem, do not weep for me, but weep for yourselves and for your children.'
The priest	We will carry our cross slowly from the back of the church, as we sing Hymn 92 'There is a Green Hill'.

The Procession

The cross is carried slowly to the altar and flanked by the candles

Jesus is nailed to the Cross

Two children bring forward the hammer and the nails

Reader	Two criminals were also led away to be put to death with Jesus. And when they came to the place of the Skull, there they crucified Him – and the criminals, one on the right and one on the left. And Jesus said, 'Father forgive them; for they know not what they do.' And the people stood by watching.
The priest	We are watching too – we're standing with the soldiers and the Jews, looking at Jesus on the Cross. But we know something they do not. We know that Jesus' terrible death is going to put everything right. It is going to save us from evil and from death.

Hymn 93 'Were you there when they crucified my Lord?' verses 1 and 2.

Children's Liturgy for Good Friday

The sponge and reed

A child brings the sponge on the reed forward

Reader   After this, Jesus said, 'I thirst!'
There was a bowl of sour wine standing there and the soldiers put a sponge full of it on a stick – and held it to Jesus' mouth.

The child puts the sponge and reed on the altar

Jesus dies on the Cross

The priest   It was now about the sixth hour, and there was darkness over the whole land until the ninth hour, for the sun stopped shining.
Then Jesus crying out with a loud voice, said,
'Father, into Thy hands I commit my spirit!'
And having said this He breathed His last.

There is a short silence as everybody kneels

And when the centurion saw what had taken place, he praised God and said, 'Truly, this man was the Son of God!'

Hymn 93 'Were you there when the sun refused to shine?' verse 4.

The Veneration of the Cross

The priest explains how one venerates the Cross and gives the children the option to kiss the Cross – or to touch it, to genuflect or just to bow the head. Ask some adults or teenagers to go first

Have some music playing as the Cross is venerated, or sing a hymn

The priest   Today we have remembered Jesus' death. This is a very sad and solemn day – but it is only the beginning of the story. Jesus did not stay dead.
What happened?

Take all answers

He came back to life. Let's remember that as we sing our last hymn.

End with the Good Friday Blessing

Children's Mass

We stand when the bell rings

THE WELCOME

> We make the **Sign of the Cross**.
> ✛ In the Name of the Father,
> and of the Son,
> and of the Holy Spirit. **Amen.**

The priest welcomes us all and tells us about today's Service
Then we say sorry to God for anything we have done wrong

> Lord, you forgive those
> who admit they are wrong.
> Lord have mercy.
> **Lord have mercy.**
>
> We are sorry for the times
> we have been unloving, selfish and unthankful.
> Christ have mercy.
> **Christ have mercy.**
>
> Lord, you show us how
> we should forgive others.
> Lord have mercy.
> **Lord have mercy.**
>
> May God ✛ forgive you all that you have done wrong,
> and bring you His joy and peace,
> through Jesus Christ our Lord. **Amen.**

THE GLORIA

> 1 Glory in the highest to the God of Heaven!
>   Peace to all your people through the Earth be given:
>   Mighty God and Father, thanks and praise we bring,
>   Singing Alleluyas to our Heavenly King.

2 Jesus Christ is risen, God the Father's Son:
    With the Holy Spirit, you are Lord alone!
  Lamb once killed for sinners, all our guilt to bear,
    Show us now your mercy, now receive our prayer.

3 Christ the world's true Saviour, high and Holy One,
    Seated now and reigning from your Father's throne:
  Lord and God, we praise you, highest Heaven adores:
    In the Father's glory, all the praise be yours!

READINGS

We hear some passages from the Bible, they end with

THE GOSPEL

Alleluia! Alleluia! Alleluia!
Alleluia! Alleluia! Alleluia!

Hear the Gospel + of Our Lord Jesus Christ
according to ....
Glory to you, O Lord.

At the end of the Gospel

This is the Gospel of the Lord.
Praise to you, O Christ.

THE SERMON

The priest gives a talk about the Gospel

This is followed by

THE CREED

Let us profess the faith of the Church.
Do you believe and trust in God the Father?
**I believe in God the Father Almighty,
Creator of Heaven and Earth.**

Do you believe and trust in His Son Jesus Christ?
**I believe in Jesus Christ, His only Son, our Lord,
who was conceived by the Holy Spirit,
born of the Virgin Mary,
suffered under Pontius Pilate,
was crucified, died and was buried.**

He descended to the dead.
On the third day He rose again,
He ascended into Heaven,
He is seated at the right hand of the Father,
and He will come to judge the living and the dead.

Do you believe and trust in the Holy Spirit?
I believe in the Holy Spirit,
the holy catholic Church,
the communion of saints,
the forgiveness of sins,
+ the resurrection of the body,
and the life everlasting. Amen.

THE PRAYERS

We pray for the church, the world and each other
After each prayer, the priest says

      Lord, in your mercy:

and we reply

      Hear our prayer.

Stand for **THE PEACE**

      The Peace of the Lord be always with you.
      And also with you.

We shake hands or hug our family and friends saying

      Peace be with you.

THE OFFERTORY

A **HYMN** *may be sung as bread and wine are brought to the Altar*
Remain standing as the priest says

> The Lord be with you.
> **And also with you.**
>
> Lift up your hearts.
> **We lift them to the Lord.**
>
> Let us give thanks to the Lord our God.
> **It is right to give thanks and praise.**

THE EUCHARISTIC PRAYER

> God, our loving Father,
> we are glad to give you thanks and praise
> because you love us,
> and gave us this great and beautiful world.
> For such great love we thank you,
> and with all the Angels and Saints we praise you singing:
>
> **Holy! Holy! Holy! Lord, God of power and might!**
> **Heaven and Earth are full of your glory.**
> **Hosanna in the highest!**
>
> **Blessèd is He who comes in the Name of the Lord.**
> **Hosanna in the highest!**
>
> Blessèd be Jesus, whom you sent to be our Friend.
> He came to show us how we can love you, Father,
> by loving each other.
> God our Father, we now ask you to send your Holy Spirit
> to change these gifts of bread and wine
> into the Body and Blood of Jesus Christ.
>
> The night before He died,
> Jesus, your Son, showed how much you loved us.
> When He was at supper with His Disciples,
> He took bread
> and gave you thanks and praise.
> Then He broke the bread
> and gave it to His Disciples saying:

160   Children's Mass

    Take, eat, this is my Body
    which is given for you
    do this in remembrance of me. +

The priest holds up the Bread of Christ's Body as a bell rings three times

DING! DING! DING!

    When supper was ended,
    Jesus took the cup that was filled with wine.
    He thanked you,
    and gave it to His Disciples saying:
    drink this, all of you
    this is my Blood of the New Covenant
    which is shed for you and for many
    for the forgiveness of sins.
    do this as often as you drink it
    in remembrance of me. +

The priest holds up the wine of Christ's Blood as a bell rings three times

DONG! DONG! DONG!

    Let us proclaim the Mystery of Faith:

Christ has died!
Christ has risen!
Christ will come again!

    And so, loving Father,
    we remember that Jesus died
    and rose again to save the world.

Remember, Father, our families and friends.
Remember those who have died.
Bring them home to you
to be with you for ever in Heaven.

Gather us all into your Kingdom,
there we shall be happy for ever.
There all the friends of Jesus will sing a song of joy.

We praise you, we bless you, we thank you!
Through Him, with Him, in Him,
in the unity of the Holy Spirit,
all glory and honour is yours,
Almighty Father, for ever and ever. Amen!

THE LORD'S PRAYER

Our Father, who art in Heaven,
hallowed be thy Name.
Thy Kingdom come,
thy will be done on Earth as it is in Heaven.
Give us this day our daily bread
and forgive us our trespasses,
as we forgive those who trespass against us.
And lead us not into temptation,
but deliver us from evil.
For thine is the Kingdom,
the power and the glory,
for ever and ever. Amen.

The priest breaks the Bread and invites everyone to come to the altar

We break this Bread to share in the Body of Christ.
**Though we are many, we are one body,
because we all share in one bread.**

+ Behold the Lamb of God who takes away the sins of the world.
Blessèd are those who are called to His supper.
**Lord, I am not worthy to receive you,
but only say the Word, and I shall be healed.**

*Please come forward to receive Communion (if you normally do)
or a Blessing*

Afterwards we say together

> Lord, we have broken your Bread.
> We have received your Life.
> By the power of your Spirit
> keep us always in your love,
> through Jesus Christ our Lord. Amen.

Some **NOTICES** *may follow*

THE BLESSING

Stand

> Bow your heads and pray for God's blessing.
> May Almighty God bless you, + Father, Son and Holy Spirit.
> **Amen.**

> The Mass is ended, go in peace to love and serve the Lord.
> **In the Name of Christ. Amen!**

The children may gather around a statue of Mary and baby Jesus to say or sing

> Hail, Mary, full of grace, the Lord is with thee;
> blessèd art thou among women,
> and blessèd is the fruit of thy womb, Jesus.
> Holy Mary, Mother of God,
> pray for us sinners now
> and at the hour of our death. Amen.

Or you may light a candle

lighting a candle can also be a prayer...

Intercessions

Intercessions for Advent

Let us pray to God our Father.
We pray for Christ's church this Advent.
For the courage to be steadfast.
For the will to live in harmony.
And for the Holy Spirit to fill all Christians with hope.
Lord, in your mercy: **hear our prayer.**
We pray for the world God has made and loves.
For peace between nations and within them.
For everyone who exercises power.
For justice and God's mercy to be seen throughout creation.
Lord, in your mercy: **hear our prayer.**
We pray for this community.
For generous and hospitable hearts.
For willing and active hands.
For pleasure in all the gifts you give us, and joy in sharing them with those we meet.
Lord, in your mercy: **hear our prayer.**
We pray for all who suffer.
For victims of violence.
For our friends in need of healing.
For everyone who needs to know your comfort and your love.
Lord, in your mercy: **hear our prayer.**
We pray for those who have died.
For their welcome into your kingdom, and for our hope that we will join them there.
For ...., who have died recently.
For .... (*insert names from sheet*) whose anniversaries are at this time.
Rest eternal grant unto them, O Lord, **and let light perpetual shine upon them.**
May they rest in peace. **Amen.**

We join our prayers with the whole host of heaven, and say:
Merciful Father, accept these prayers for the sake of Your Son, Our Saviour Jesus Christ. Amen.

Intercessions for Christmas

Father, the whole world is full of your goodness.
We pray for everyone who cares for the planet and its animals.
Help us to keep the earth healthy and beautiful.
Lord, in your mercy: **hear our prayer.**
Father, every human person is made in your image.
We pray for people who are scared or angry, and for people who fight wars and hurt others.
Help us to make peace.
Lord, in your mercy: **hear our prayer.**
Father, you sent Jesus to show us what love is and be our brother.
We pray for Christians, who try to show that love to others.
Help us to follow Jesus by being patient and forgiving.
Lord, in your mercy: **hear our prayer.**
Father, Jesus' family was poor and in danger.
We pray for all children who are spending Christmas without family, food or presents.
Help us not to be greedy.
Lord, in your mercy: **hear our prayer.**
Father, Jesus is the most wonderful gift.
We pray that we will come to know him better and better.
Help us to grow closer to you and to be happy.
All the angels in heaven bow down before Jesus, who is God made man. May the Holy Spirit be in us as we pray:
Merciful Father, accept these prayers for the sake of Your Son, Our Saviour Jesus Christ. Amen.

Intercessions for Candlemas

Let us pray to the Father through Christ who is our light and life.
Father, Jesus Christ is the true light and the glory of Israel.
Help the church to spread the light of Christ wherever it is found.
Lord, in your mercy: **hear our prayer.**

Pause

Father, Jesus came to bring hope to every nation.
Be close to everyone in power, in this country and abroad.
And bring safety where there is danger.
Lord, in your mercy: **hear our prayer.**

Pause

Father, Jesus depended on his family as he grew up.
Teach us to depend on one another.
Lord, in your mercy: **hear our prayer.**

Pause

Father, Jesus became poor for our sakes:
Comfort the poor and the sick who suffer with Him.
Lord, in your mercy: **hear our prayer.**

Pause

Father, Simeon and Anna found peace in Jesus Christ.
Give everyone who has died your salvation and your peace.
Lord, in your mercy: **hear our prayer.**
We join our prayers with those of all the saints and angels.
**Merciful Father, accept these prayers for the sake of Your Son,
Our Saviour Jesus Christ. Amen.**

Intercessions for Any Saint

Let us pray to God our Father in heaven.
God, your Spirit gave the saints [*or:* St N] courage.
Fill Christians everywhere with your Spirit, and make them bold
and strong.
Lord, in your mercy: **hear our prayer.**
In the life of the saints [*or:* St N] we see what joy looks like.
Give your joy to everyone who is anxious or self-centred.
Lord, in your mercy: **hear our prayer.**
The saints [*or:* St N] brought good news to their/his/her
neighbours.
Help us to say only things that are kind and true.
Lord, in your mercy: **hear our prayer.**
The saints [*or:* St N] were/was not afraid to die, because they/he/
she trusted you.

Bring everyone who has died to join the saints in heaven.
Lord, in your mercy: **hear our prayer.**
In heaven, the saints [*or:* St N] pray[s] for the whole world and everything in it.
Teach us to pray on earth as the saints do in heaven.
Lord, in your mercy: **hear our prayer.**
Joining our prayers with the prayers of the Blessed Virgin Mary [*or:* St N], and all the saints, we say:
Merciful Father, accept these prayers for the sake of Your Son, Our Saviour Jesus Christ. Amen.

Intercessions for Baptism of the Lord

In the power of the Spirit and in Union with Christ, let us pray to the Father.
Father, wash us with the water of Baptism.
Wash away our mistakes and our selfishness.
Make us ready to begin a fresh new life each day.
Lord, hear us: **Lord, graciously hear us.**
Father, be close to us with your Holy Spirit.
Let us see and hear you in the sacraments and in the scriptures.
Fill the church with joy and help it grow.
Lord, hear us: **Lord, graciously hear us.**
Father, shine light into the world.
Heal people who are ashamed of themselves or violent to others.
Let everyone know the truth, that they are loved.
Lord, hear us: **Lord, graciously hear us.**
Father, show us how to live like Jesus.
Help us to be proud of knowing you.
Help us to talk about you and help others know you too.
Lord, hear us: **Lord, graciously hear us.**
Father, bless everyone who has joined Jesus in Baptism.
Thank you for keeping safe everyone who has died.
Bring everyone to join you with Jesus in heaven.
Lord, hear us: **Lord, graciously hear us.**
With the new gift of God's Spirit in our hearts, we say:
Merciful Father, accept these prayers for the sake of Your Son, Our Saviour Jesus Christ. Amen.

Intercessions for Mothering Sunday (Lent 4)

Let us pray to God our Father.

Lord, we pray for the church.
We thank you that she mothers us, and helps us to grow as children of God.
Keep the whole church safe, and strong, and happy.
Lord, in your mercy: **hear our prayer.**
Lord, we pray for Mother Earth.
We thank you that our planet gives us food, and shelter, and beauty.
Help us look after our planet, and bless those with too little.
Lord, in your mercy: **hear our prayer.**
Lord, we pray for all your children.
We thank you for the mothers who gave us life, and for all the people who have looked after us.
Take care of children and parents everywhere, especially in danger or poverty.
Lord, in your mercy: **hear our prayer.**
Lord, we pray for this church.
We thank you for everyone who helps with Crèche, and Children's Church, and Youth Church.
Teach us to be more like children in trusting you.
Lord, in your mercy: **hear our prayer.**
Lord, we pray for people who are sick.
We thank you that you love us and want us to be well.
Heal anyone who is ill or sad, and be close to the lonely.
Lord, in your mercy: **hear our prayer.**
Lord, we pray for everyone who has died.
We thank you that you keep on loving us even when we die.
Bring us all home to stay with you forever, and bless [names].
Lord, in your mercy: **hear our prayer.**
We join our prayers with the prayers of Mary the mother of Jesus, and all the holy saints and angels.
Merciful Father, accept these prayers for the sake of Your Son, Our Saviour Jesus Christ. Amen.

Intercessions for Easter

	We ask the Spirit to help us pray to God our Father.
Child 1:	Jesus burst out of the tomb.
Child 2:	Help us to burst open with joy and love, and pour happiness around.
Child 1:	Jesus opened his arms wide to hold us.
Child 2:	Bless the men and women who take care of us at home and at school.
Child 1:	Jesus trusted that he was doing what God wanted.
Child 2:	Help all Christians to trust God and do the things that please him.
Child 1:	Jesus was hurt by closed, frightened people.
Child 2:	Gently open the hearts of everyone who hurts others.
Child 1:	Jesus conquered death so that everyone could live.
Child 2:	Help us to live full lives, and bring everyone who has died to everlasting life.
Child 1:	Jesus made everything that exists, and never stops praying for the whole world.
Child 2:	We join our prayers with his.
	Merciful Father, accept these prayers for the sake of Your Son, Our Saviour Jesus Christ. Amen.

Intersessions for Ascension or for Trinity Sunday, or as a General Intercession

Heavenly Father, we love you although we cannot see you.
We see people who are sad or hurt. Help us to love them.
We see people harming one another. Help us to love peace.
We see people damaging the world. Help us to love creation.
Lord, in your mercy: **hear our prayer.**
Jesus our Brother, you loved us on earth and you love us in heaven.
You pray for us in heaven. Help us pray for others on earth.
You send us hope from heaven. Help us show your hope on earth.
You live forever in heaven. Help us live with joy on earth.
Lord, in your mercy: **hear our prayer.**
God the Spirit, you are the giver of life.
Through our prayers and our worship. Give us your life.
Through our loving friends and families. Give us your life.
You are with us at all times and in all places. Give us your life.
Lord, in your mercy: **hear our prayer.**

The saints in heaven know you perfectly and love you completely.
May we know you and love you more and more each day.
**Merciful Father, accept these prayers for the sake of Your Son,
Our Saviour Jesus Christ. Amen.**

This can be used on the Feast of the Trinity – or at any other time!

Intercessions for Pentecost

In the joy of God's Holy Spirit, let us pray with Christ to the Father.
Father, by your Spirit you made the whole world.
By your Spirit, heal the world's damage.
By your Spirit, restore the world to peace.
By your Spirit, fill the world with beauty.
Lord, in your mercy: **hear our prayer.**
Father, through your Spirit you sent Christ to save us.
By your Spirit, teach us about Jesus.
By your Spirit, make us followers of Jesus.
By your Spirit, make the church loving and strong.
Lord, in your mercy: **hear our prayer.**
Father, you sent your Spirit to comfort us.
By your Spirit, heal the sick.
By your Spirit, comfort the sad.
By your Spirit, strengthen the weak and doubting.
Lord, in your mercy: **hear our prayer.**
Father, your Spirit is the spirit of joy.
By your Spirit, make us friends with one another.
By your Spirit, give us energy and purpose.
By your Spirit, guide us in our lives.
Lord, in your mercy: **hear our prayer.**
The fruit of the Spirit is Love, Joy, Peace.
Give peace to the departed, and bring us with them to your
    joyful feasting in heaven.
**Merciful Father, accept these prayers for the sake of Your Son,
Our Saviour Jesus Christ. Amen.**

Intercessions for Holy Trinity Sunday

With Christ and in the Spirit, let us pray to God the Father.
Thank you, God, for giving us hearts to love you and minds to know you.
Help us to love you more and know you better through our prayers.
Lord, in your mercy: **hear our prayer.**
You are a mystery and you have made all human beings mysteries, too.
Teach human beings everywhere to treat each other with respect and care.
Lord, in your mercy: **hear our prayer.**
God, the whole of the universe is full of your glory.
Show us how to enjoy and protect the world we live in.
Lord, in your mercy: **hear our prayer.**
God of three in one and one in three, you are true love and relationship.
Bless those who are lonely or sad or cruel to others.
Eternal God, you live forever.
Take everyone who has died into your home in heaven, and bring us there too when we die.
Lord, in your mercy: **hear our prayer.**
We thank you that Christ prays for us
And that the Spirit prays in us.
Merciful Father, accept these prayers for the sake of Your Son, Our Saviour Jesus Christ. Amen.

Intercessions in Petertide

Let us pray.
God our Father, we thank you for gathering us together as a family.
Bless the work of the whole church, especially new priests and deacons.
Help us to be faithful Christians and serve you better.
Lord, in your mercy: **hear our prayer.**
God our Father, we thank you for making the world and everything in in it.
Bless all men, women and children who have to live with danger or violence, or without enough food or water or medicine.

Help us to remember that we are all your children, wherever we are from.
Lord, in your mercy: **hear our prayer.**
God our Father, we thank you for our friends and families, our schools and our work.
Bless all the people we see day by day and keep them safe.
Help us to show kindness to people we don't like as well as the people we do.
Lord, in your mercy: **hear our prayer.**
God our Father, we thank you for doctors and nurses to take care of us when we are ill.
Bless everyone who is sick or unhappy today, and anyone who is alone.
Help us to think about other people, and help them if we can.
Lord, in your mercy: **hear our prayer.**
God our Father, we thank you that when we die we can be with you forever.
Bless everyone who has died, especially ....
Help us to live our lives in the hope of joining you in heaven.
Lord, in your mercy: **hear our prayer.**
We ask Mary our Mother, and all the holy saints and angels to pray for us.
Merciful Father, accept these prayers for the sake of Your Son, Our Saviour Jesus Christ.

Intercessions for the Family Eucharist with Holy Baptism

Diaconate as theme of sermon

Lord God, we pray for the church in every country. Make all its bishops, priests and leaders faithful servants of the gospel. Protect all Christians in danger, and teach us to serve you and one another.
Lord, in your mercy: **hear our prayer.**
Lord God, you love the world you have made. We lift up to you all the places where people are hungry or afraid, or where lives are spoiled by war. Help us to be kind to the planet and generous to anyone in need.
Lord, in your mercy: **hear our prayer.**
Lord God, we ask you to bless our church, our schools, and our homes and families. We pray especially for [Name] and [Name]

as they join our Christian family through baptism today. Bring all your children closer together in love and service.
Lord, in your mercy: **hear our prayer.**
Lord God, your Son Jesus healed many sick people. Heal and strengthen everyone who is ill, especially ....
Give courage to the doctors, nurses, and carers who look after them.
Lord, in your mercy: **hear our prayer.**
Lord God, we remember your servants who have died, among them ....
We thank you that their names are written in heaven, and pray that our names will be written there too.
Rest eternal grant unto them, O Lord, and let light perpetual shine upon them. May they rest in peace.
Lord, in your mercy: **hear our prayer.**
We pray along with the Blessed Virgin Mary, St Michael and all the angels and saints:
Merciful Father, accept these prayers for the sake of Your Son, Our Saviour Jesus Christ. Amen.

Intercessions for Harvest

Let us pray to God our Father.
Father, we pray for the church throughout the world, and for the safety of all Christians.
We thank you for our daily bread, and for feeding us with the sacraments.
We ask you to make all the church's work fruitful.
Lord, in your mercy: **hear our prayer.**
Father, we pray for the earth and everything in it, and especially for people who produce and transport food.
We thank you for people who are working to end hunger.
We ask you to protect the men, women and children who will still go hungry today.
Lord, in your mercy: **hear our prayer.**
Father, we pray for the restaurants, markets and shops of this parish, and all who work in them.
We thank you for everyone who offers hospitality and for the ministry of hospitality in this church.
We ask you to help us share what we have and think of the needs of other people.

Lord, in your mercy: **hear our prayer.**
Father, we pray for everyone who is ill, upset or afraid today.
We thank you for our friends, neighbours and colleagues and
everyone who takes care of others.
We ask you to make your love known to everyone in any kind
of need.
Lord, in your mercy: **hear our prayer.**
Father, we pray for everyone who has died and for everyone who
is mourning.
We thank you for your promise that we can join your feast
in heaven.
We ask you to bless .... who have died recently; and ....
whose anniversary of death falls at this time.
Lord, in your mercy: **hear our prayer.**
We ask Our Lady, St Michael and all the saints and angels to pray
for us.
**Merciful Father, accept these prayers for the sake of Your Son,
Our Saviour Jesus Christ. Amen.**

Intercessions invoking the prayers of the Virgin Mary – suitable for Assumption or any Marian feast

Let us pray with Mary and all the saints to God our Father
in heaven.
For everyone who loves Jesus, your Son, and tries to follow him
and act like him:
We pray, and Mary prays too.
Lord, in your mercy: **hear our prayer.**
For the people who are left out, or left behind, or bullied, or lonely:
We pray, and Mary prays too.
Lord, in your mercy: **hear our prayer.**
For powerful people, and people with big responsibilities
and worries:
We pray, and Mary prays too.
Lord, in your mercy: **hear our prayer.**
For people who are dying, and for the friends and family who
love them:
We pray, and Mary prays too.
Lord, in your mercy: **hear our prayer.**

For all your children, even when they have died and left this life.
We pray, and Mary prays too.
Lord, in your mercy: **hear our prayer.**
For ourselves, because we would like to know heaven and be close to you.
We pray, and Mary prays too.
Lord, in your mercy: **hear our prayer.**
Holy Mary, Mother of God, pray for us now and at the hour of our death.
Merciful Father, accept these prayers for the sake of Your Son, Our Saviour Jesus Christ. Amen.

General Intercessions

Let us pray to God, our loving Father, who is always pleased to hear us.
Father, we thank you for the gift of baptism.
Guard all Christians everywhere, and keep them true to their promises.
Help us to grow more and more like Jesus our brother, in faith and hope and love.
Lord, in your mercy: **hear our prayer.**
Father, we thank you for the beauty of the world and for every human life you have made.
Bless all the families and communities and countries that make up the world.
Help all people to love creation, bring peace, and show mercy, as Jesus did.
Lord, in your mercy: **hear our prayer.**
Father, we thank you for our city, our church, our homes and schools, our offices and parks.
Protect the people who live and work around us, and bring goodness out of all our activities.
Help us to remember that Jesus died for all your children, and that we are all equal in your eyes.
Lord, in your mercy: **hear our prayer.**
Father, we thank you for our health and for the pleasure we can take in life.
Heal those who are ill, comfort those who are in pain, and
strengthen anyone who is tired or sad, especially those we know.

Pause

Help us to follow Jesus by visiting and caring for people in need.
Lord, in your mercy: **hear our prayer.**
Father, we thank you that you promise everlasting life to everyone who believes in your Son.
Bless all those who have died, among them .... [*list names*].
Help us all to be worthy to join Jesus in heaven.
Lord, in your mercy: **hear our prayer.**
We join our prayers with those of the Blessed Virgin Mary, St Michael and all the holy angels and saints, saying:
Merciful Father, accept these prayers for the sake of Your Son, Our Saviour Jesus Christ. Amen.

General Intercessions (with reference to doctors and artists)

Let us pray to God our Father.
Father in heaven,
We thank you for the gift of your Son, Jesus Christ.
Bless all Christians, especially those who are persecuted.
Help us to live in the way that Christ shows us.
Lord, in your mercy: **hear our prayer.**
Father in heaven,
We thank you for the gift of enough to eat.
Bless those who are hungry or cold, homeless or struggling.
Help us to remember that you love everyone equally, wherever they are.
Lord, in your mercy: **hear our prayer.**
Father in heaven,
We thank you for the gift of beauty and pleasure.
Bless artists and musicians and chefs, and all who work to make life beautiful.
Help us to share all your good gifts with all our brothers and sisters.
Lord, in your mercy: **hear our prayer.**
Father in heaven,
We thank you for the gifts of health and medicine.
Bless everyone who is ill, or suffering pain or sadness today.
Help us to live our lives to the full, and to take care of our bodies properly.
Lord, in your mercy: **hear our prayer.**

Father in heaven,
We thank you for the gift of eternal life.
Bless all those who have died, especially ....
Help us to believe your promises and live in the hope of heaven.

Intercessions for the Church and the Community

Let us pray to God our Father.
Heavenly Father, help the church.
Help it grow bigger.
Help it grow in courage when it is in danger.
Help all of us to grow more like Christ, and become saints like your saints in heaven.
Lord, in your mercy: **hear our prayer.**
Heavenly Father, help the world.
Help the earth to flourish and help us look after it.
Help all governments to act with good sense.
Help people in every country to work for peace, and raise up new saints.
Lord, in your mercy: **hear our prayer.**
Heavenly Father, help this community.
Help us worship you faithfully.
Help us take joy in one another and all your gifts.
Help us show kindness to everyone we meet, even if they are not like us.
Lord, in your mercy: **hear our prayer.**

Intercessions with Holy Baptism

Father in heaven,
We thank you that you have called us by name, and made us your own.
Bless all Christians across the world,
And especially [Name] and [Name] as they are baptized.

Pause

Lord, in your mercy: **hear our prayer.**
Father in heaven,
We thank you for loving everything you have made.
Help all men and women to work for peace,
And to protect the planet from harm.

Pause

Lord, in your mercy: **hear our prayer.**
Father in heaven,
We thank you for this church and for everyone who worships you here.
Make us kind and gentle to each other,
And loving to people we meet.

Pause

Lord, in your mercy: **hear our prayer.**
Father in heaven,
We thank you for sending Jesus to heal the sick.
Comfort everyone who is ill
And strengthen the people who take care of them.

Pause

Lord, in your mercy: **hear our prayer.**
Father in heaven,
We thank you that you have made a home for us in heaven with you.
Bless all those who have died
And bring them into your presence.
Today we pray for .... (*names*)

Pause

Lord, in your mercy: **hear our prayer.**
We ask the Blessed Virgin Mary,
And all the holy saints and angels,
to pray for us and everyone in need.
Merciful Father, accept these prayers for the sake of Your Son, Our Saviour Jesus Christ. Amen.

Stations of the Cross

A station is a place where you stop, and in many churches there are 14 pictures hung on the wall at which people stop to pray. They tell the story of Jesus' last journey as He carried His Cross through Jerusalem to the hill outside, where He would be crucified.

Today we will be going round with the children, looking at each picture, joining in the story, and saying a prayer before we move on to the next.

Some churches have a 15th picture, the Resurrection. But the best way to hear that story is to come back on Easter Sunday and join in the celebration of Jesus' triumph over death. (We roll a few Easter eggs down the aisle as well.)

1 PILATE CONDEMNS JESUS

Kneel

+ We adore you, O Christ, and we bless you.
Because by your holy Cross you have saved the world.

Stand up

Jesus has been arrested. He has done nothing wrong but His judge, Pontius Pilate, is too scared to let Him go free. He washes his hands to show he doesn't want anything to do with Jesus – and condemns Him to death anyway.

We wash our hands in the Roman fashion, by pouring water into a bowl over somebody's hands

As we think of Jesus unjustly condemned to death we say:

Lord have mercy.
Lord have mercy.
Christ have mercy.
Christ have mercy.
Lord have mercy.
Lord have mercy.

2 JESUS CARRIES HIS CROSS

Kneel

+ We adore you, O Christ, and we bless you.
Because by your holy Cross you have saved the world.

Stand up

The Roman soldiers put a heavy cross on Jesus' back. He will carry it up the main street, all the way through Jerusalem, to a hill outside the city.

Show the children a wooden cross

This is only a small one, but it's still quite heavy.
Let's make the Sign of the Cross together.

**+ In the Name of the Father,
and of the Son,
and of the Holy Spirit.
Amen.**

3 JESUS FALLS THE FIRST TIME

Kneel

+ We adore you, O Christ, and we bless you.
Because by your holy Cross you have saved the world.

Stand up

The Cross is so heavy that Jesus stumbles …

The children fall on one knee

We say the Jesus prayer together.

**Lord Jesus Christ, Son of God.
Have mercy on me, a sinner.
Amen.**

4 JESUS MEETS HIS MOTHER

Kneel

+ We adore you, O Christ, and we bless you.
Because by your holy Cross you have saved the world.

Stand up

Jesus' mother Mary is in the crowd and for a moment mother and Son look at each other. Jesus knew that His mother loved Him, right up to the end. Mothers always love their children. How do you know your mum loves you? She hugs you – like this …

One of the parents puts their arm round their child

That's what Mary did. Let us ask Mary to pray for us.

Hail Mary, full of grace, the Lord is with thee,
blessed art thou among women,
and blessed is the fruit of thy womb, Jesus.

**Holy Mary, Mother of God,
pray for us sinners now, and at the hour of our death.
Amen.**

5 SIMON OF CYRENE HELPS JESUS CARRY THE CROSS

Kneel

+ We adore you, O Christ, and we bless you.
Because by your holy Cross you have saved the world.

Stand up

The Cross is too heavy for Jesus to carry, so the Roman soldiers tell a man in the crowd to help Him. His name was Simon, he was a foreigner and came from Cyrene. Ever since the first Good Friday Christians have wanted to be like Simon and help Jesus carry His Cross. Jesus said that anyone who followed Him should be ready to carry a cross – can we do it?

Some children hold the wooden cross together

Take up the Cross, our Saviour said,
If you would my disciple be;
Deny yourself, the world forsake,
And humbly follow after me.

Help us to follow you, Lord. Amen.

6 VERONICA WIPES THE FACE OF JESUS

Kneel

+ We adore you, O Christ, and we bless you.
Because by your holy Cross you have saved the world.

Stand up

One of the women in the crowd came forward and wiped Jesus' face with a napkin.

A child unfolds a napkin

Her name was Veronica. It's good to know that on this last journey people still loved Jesus, and wanted to be kind to Him. When Veronica looked at her napkin she found a copy of Jesus' face on the cloth. We pray that one day we will see Jesus' face.

God be gracious to us and bless us.
And cause His face to shine upon us.
Amen.

7 JESUS FALLS THE SECOND TIME

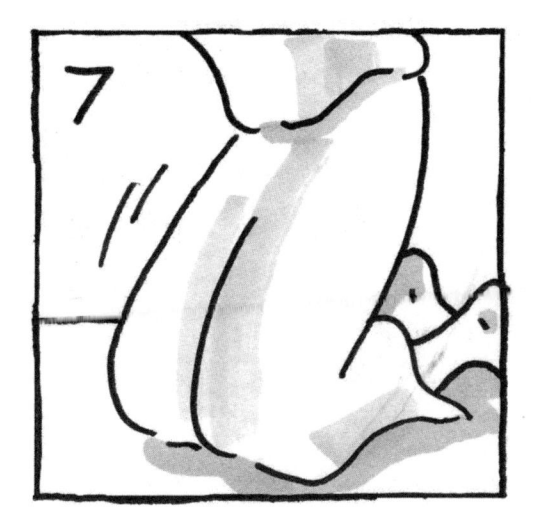

Kneel

+ We adore you, O Christ, and we bless you.
Because by your holy Cross you have saved the world.

Stand up

Even with Simon's help, Jesus is too weak to carry the Cross. He falls again.

The children fall on both knees

Jesus isn't just carrying a wooden cross, He's carrying all the things people have done wrong. The sins of the world are piled up on His back, no wonder He falls down. But it doesn't stop Him loving us.

Praise the Lord for His great kindness.
For His love lasts for ever.
Amen.

8 JESUS MEETS THE WOMEN OF JERUSALEM

Kneel

+ We adore you, O Christ, and we bless you.
Because by your holy Cross you have saved the world.

Stand up

This is the moment when people like us join the story.
Jesus passed a crowd of mothers with their children, some of them were crying – and Jesus found time to tell them He loved them. He never forgot that God His Father is our Father too.
We're going to show that we are one family by putting our hands together …

The children put their hands together

… and saying the first part of the prayer that Jesus taught us.

**Our Father, who art in Heaven,
Hallowed be thy Name.
Thy Kingdom come,
They will be done, on Earth as it is in Heaven.
Amen.**

9 JESUS FALLS THE THIRD TIME

Kneel

+ We adore you, O Christ, and we bless you.
Because by your holy Cross you have saved the world.

Stand up

Jesus falls for the third time, but it doesn't matter now. He has reached the end of His journey. How far can you fall?

The children fall in any way they like

OK, that's good. Sit up for a minute …
Jesus didn't get up as quickly as you, He lay there, on the earth, praying to His Father. Let's finish the prayer He taught us.

**Give us this day our daily bread,
And forgive us our trespasses,
As we forgive those who trespass against us.
And lead us not into temptation,
But deliver us from evil.
For thine is the Kingdom, the power and the glory,
For ever and ever. Amen.**

10 JESUS IS STRIPPED OF HIS GARMENTS

Kneel

+ We adore you, O Christ, and we bless you.
Because by your holy Cross you have saved the world.

Stand up

When Jesus came down to Earth, He left everything behind, His Father, and the angels, and His home in heaven.
And He didn't mind, because He loved us so much.
Now He's got nothing left – the soldiers have even taken His clothes – but that's fine. He's prepared to give away everything, as long as He can save us. Is there anything we can give Jesus?

Throw it open, anything the children say will be interesting

Let's end by saying part of a carol we sing at Christmas.

What can I give Him? Poor as I am.
If I were a shepherd, I would bring a lamb.
If I were a wise man, I would do my part.
But what I can I give Him – give my heart.

11 CRUCIFIXION: JESUS IS NAILED TO THE CROSS

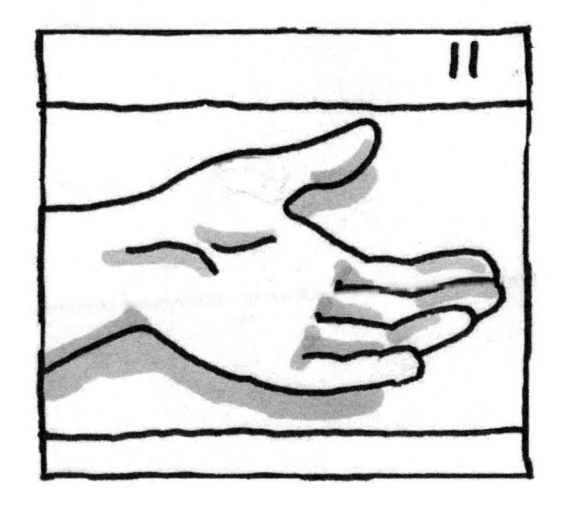

Kneel

+ We adore you, O Christ, and we bless you.
Because by your holy Cross you have saved the world.

Stand up

Nobody likes this station. It's time to be gentle, and quiet.

The children sit down

Sometimes, when things are horrible, it helps to listen to music, or sing quietly. Let's do that.

**There is a green hill far away,
Without a city wall,
Where the dear Lord was crucified,
Who died to save us all.**

**He died that we may be forgiven,
He died to make us good;
That we might go at last to Heaven,
Saved by His precious blood.**

12 JESUS DIES ON THE CROSS

Kneel

+ We adore you, O Christ, and we bless you.
Because by your holy Cross you have saved the world.

Everybody remains kneeling for the Gospel

It was now about noon, and darkness came over the whole land until three in the afternoon, as the sun's light failed. Then Jesus, crying with a loud voice, said 'Father, into your hands I commend my spirit.' Having said this, He breathed His last.
St Luke 23.46

We sit to sing

Were you there when they crucified my Lord?
Were you there when they crucified my Lord?
Oh, sometimes it causes me to tremble, tremble, tremble;
Were you there when they crucified my Lord?

Were you there when the sun refused to shine?
Were you there when the sun refused to shine?
Oh, sometimes it causes me to tremble, tremble, tremble;
Were you there when the sun refused to shine?

13 JESUS IS TAKEN DOWN FROM THE CROSS

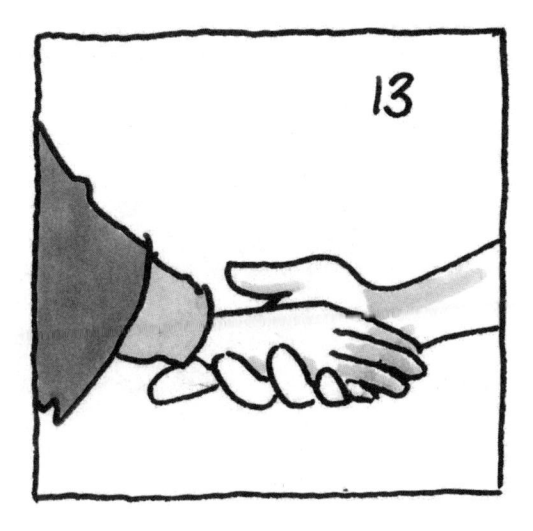

Kneel

+ We adore you, O Christ, and we bless you.
Because by your holy Cross you have saved the world.

Stand up

It's over. Jesus' body is taken down from the Cross and, at last, His mother can hold Him in her arms. It's good to touch the people we love, and to hold their hand … We do that in church by giving each other the Sign of Peace.

Everyone shakes hands with each other as they say

Peace be with you.
And also with you.

14 JESUS IS LAID IN THE TOMB

Kneel

+ We adore you, O Christ, and we bless you.
Because by your holy Cross you have saved the world.

Stand up

Good Friday ends very quietly, with Jesus being laid to rest in the Tomb. But He won't be there very long …
Can anyone show me how one starts a race?

A child adopts a crouching position

Anyone else able to do that?

The other children crouch down

OK, get ready, Jesus is in His Tomb – all through Friday – are you still ready? – all through Saturday – He was getting ready too – and on the third day – wait for it – He jumped to his feet!

The kids jump up

But we'll have to wait until Easter Sunday for that. We'll say one last prayer together.

Let us bless the Lord.
Thanks be to God.
Amen.